**New Directions for
Community Colleges**

Arthur M. Cohen
EDITOR-IN-CHIEF

Richard L. Wagoner
ASSOCIATE EDITOR

Allison Kanny
MANAGING EDITOR

MW00413622

The Community College in a Global Context

Tod Treat
Linda Serra Hagedorn
EDITORS

Number 161 • Spring 2013
Jossey-Bass
San Francisco

THE COMMUNITY COLLEGE IN A GLOBAL CONTEXT
Tod Treat and Linda Serra Hagedorn (eds.)
New Directions for Community Colleges, no. 161

Arthur M. Cohen, Editor-in-Chief
Richard L. Wagoner, Associate Editor
Allison Kanny, Managing Editor

NEW DIRECTIONS FOR COMMUNITY COLLEGES (ISSN 0194-3081, electronic ISSN 1536-0733) is part of The Jossey-Bass Higher and Adult Education Series and is published quarterly by Wiley Subscription Services, Inc., A Wiley Company, at Jossey-Bass, One Montgomery St., Ste. 1200, San Francisco, CA 94104. Periodicals Postage Paid at San Francisco, California, and at additional mailing offices. POSTMASTER: Send address changes to New Directions for Community Colleges, Jossey-Bass, One Montgomery St., Ste. 1200, San Francisco, CA 94104.

SUBSCRIPTIONS cost $89 for individuals in the U.S., Canada, and Mexico, and $113 in the rest of the world for print only; $89 in all regions for electronic only; $98 in the U.S., Canada, and Mexico for combined print and electronic; $122 for combined print and electronic in the rest of the world. Institutional print only subscriptions are $292 in the U.S, $332 in Canada and Mexico, and $366 in the rest of the world; electronic only subscriptions are $292 in all regions; combined print and electronic subscriptions are $335 in the U.S. and $375 in Canada and Mexico.

EDITORIAL CORRESPONDENCE should be sent to the Editor-in-Chief, Arthur M. Cohen, at the Graduate School of Education and Information Studies, University of California, Box 951521, Los Angeles, CA 90095-1521. All manuscripts receive anonymous reviews by external referees.

New Directions for Community Colleges is indexed in CIJE: Current Index to Journals in Education (ERIC), Contents Pages in Education (T&F), Current Abstracts (EBSCO), Ed/Net (Simpson Communications), Education Index/Abstracts (H. W. Wilson), Educational Research Abstracts Online (T&F), ERIC Database (Education Resources Information Center), and Resources in Education (ERIC).

Microfilm copies of issues and articles are available in 16mm and 35mm, as well as microfiche in 105mm, through University Microfilms Inc., 300 North Zeeb Road, Ann Arbor, MI 48106-1346.

CONTENTS

EDITORS' NOTES

The purpose of this volume of *New Directions for Community Colleges* is to explore the community college in an international context in an effort to address the needs and interests of both scholars in the field and leaders on the front line of educating students in a globalized world. The contributors to this volume are deeply committed to the essential work of community colleges *in the world*, simultaneously addressing global ideals, values, competencies, and understanding in a local context.

In Chapter 1, we resituate the U.S. community college in a global context. Our premise, which is supported throughout the volume, is that international education is core to our mission, that the community college is rapidly becoming less about the United States and more about *all of us*. Internationalization through people, planning, and partnerships has a dramatic impact on learning, on workforce preparation, and, in a few notable cases, on burgeoning democratic identities worldwide.

Chapters 2 and 3 provide models for planning and implementing international education. Bonnie Bissonette and Shawn Woodin provide a model for enhancing internationalization at community colleges that attempts to address both the community college context and a developmental approach that moves from isolated to integrated activities. In addition, community colleges should work to develop leadership support beginning with the board of trustees and executive leadership. Michael Brennan and Donald A. Dellow provide a rationale for comprehensive internationalization and create a sense of urgency, illustrating that, if community colleges fail to integrate international education as a core element, they do so to the detriment of their communities and their students.

Chapters 4 and 5 present cases of transformational institutional internationalization. Geoffrey Bradshaw details an "arc of community college internationalization" that leverages regional consortia, obtains external funding to achieve staffing and infrastructure development, generates credibility through continuous assessment and improvement, and builds capacity and involvement of faculty in field studies and service learning to create experiential learning experiences for students. Jack Bermingham and Margaret. Ryan provide insight into the Highline Community College strategy for internationalization, which couples deep professional development of faculty and staff and wide-ranging international development projects to transform an institution.

In Chapter 6, Tod Treat and Mary Beth Hartenstine outline a model for strategic partnerships in which resource needs, purpose-driven approaches, cultural dimensions, and social network dimensions all play a role in deter-

New Directions for Community Colleges, no. 161, Spring 2013 © 2013 Wiley Periodicals, Inc.
Published online in Wiley Online Library (wileyonlinelibrary.com) • DOI: 10.1002/cc.20043

mining what partnerships to prioritize, how to assess their success, and how to sustain them.

Chapters 7, 8, and 9 move the focus to developments outside the United States that so dramatically affect the future of international education in community colleges. Anh T. Le outlines the growth and progression of the burgeoning community college system in Vietnam. Linda Serra Hagedorn and Wafa Thabet Mezghani address efforts to bring community colleges to Tunisia, outlining the specific cultural attributes that must be considered for successful adaptation of the community college model. The important efforts in these two countries are but a few of a host of non-U.S. community college systems now in development, illustrating both the recognition internationally of the effectiveness of the model and the deep responsibility of us all to provide support and partnership.

The final chapter of the volume presents a broader perspective addressing the potential impact of community college adoption in the Middle East and North Africa. In Chapter 9, John Shumaker of AMIDEAST suggests that three systemic issues must be addressed as community college models are considered: levels of institutional autonomy, leadership, and student access and enrollment flexibility. Institutionally, these issues are manifest in the degree of stakeholder engagement, level of focus on student success, balance of theory and practice, and methods of teaching and learning.

In the end, this volume's reflection on how individual community colleges have internationalized, how models and partnerships can aid progression to comprehensive internationalization, and how international systems consider adoption and adaptation points to a crucial vision for the future: Globalization has moved the U.S. community college steadily from international education as add-on to international education as a choice, and now to international education as a crucial, integrated mission that has drawn increased interest from other nations intent on an educated and skilled citizenry. The community college is no longer about the United States; the community college is for *all of us*, a world phenomenon.

Our appreciation goes out to the authors for their commitment to this international work and for sharing that work through this volume. As with all editorial work, the twists and turns needed to finalize the volume required patience and quick responses on the part of the authors, for which we are grateful. Finally, we wish to thank the editors of *New Directions for Community Colleges* for their continued commitment to bridging research and practice and for offering a venue for dialogue and professional development that advances the community college mission.

Tod Treat
Linda Serra Hagedorn
Editors

NEW DIRECTIONS FOR COMMUNITY COLLEGES • DOI: 10.1002/cc

TOD TREAT is vice president for Student and Academic Services at Richland Community College in Decatur, Illinois, and adjunct assistant professor in the Department of Education Policy, Organization, and Leadership at the University of Illinois at Urbana–Champaign.

LINDA SERRA HAGEDORN is professor and associate dean in the College of Human Sciences at Iowa State University in Ames, Iowa.

NEW DIRECTIONS FOR COMMUNITY COLLEGES • DOI: 10.1002/cc

1

From locally focused institutions intent on access and affordability to higher education, workforce preparation, and community engagement, the contemporary community college is poised as a global partner for the democratization and development of a global workforce.

Resituating the Community College in a Global Context

Tod Treat, Linda Serra Hagedorn

Community colleges were never designed to be international education centers. In fact, colleges were renamed "community" in lieu of "junior" to specifically highlight the college's role in serving the needs of the local community. Community colleges' missions have been traditionally locally focused: meeting the needs of students in transfer, career and technical, developmental, and community education. Importantly, community colleges have had the responsibility to train the community citizenry to meet the needs of local employers, thus creating local workforce development for economic prosperity. Many community college systems contain a local element of funding, such as local property taxes or sales taxes. At the same time, community colleges have historically focused on access, affordability, and convenience that have served their geographic service areas well.

Community needs and demands have driven community colleges to enhance instructional delivery to accommodate busy lifestyles coupled with economic downturns and uncertainties; to build new partnerships; to expand outreach; and to create systems that are highly innovative, flexible, and adaptive. Community colleges have also developed capability to effectively utilize technology for learning, including learning management systems and social media.

The world of the 21st century is very different from what existed when community colleges were established. Today, postsecondary institutions of all kinds can no longer be insulated from global concerns. Nor can students be educated without at least some global knowledge and the expectation of

New Directions for Community Colleges, no. 161, Spring 2013 © 2013 Wiley Periodicals, Inc.
Published online in Wiley Online Library (wileyonlinelibrary.com) • DOI: 10.1002/cc.20044

living in a globalized environment. There is an acute need for increased access to relevant, responsive, socioeconomically progressive international education. The community college is uniquely situated to pivot as a key global partner for the democratization and development of a global workforce. In this introductory chapter to this volume, we revisit the development of international education in the community college and posit that U.S. community colleges, and the community college model in general, are poised to play a crucial role in the evolving global economic, social, and educational environment, should we meet the challenge.

Community College International Education in Three Acts

The concept of a "flat" globalized world in which technological and economic interconnectivity leads to a reduced state or geographical isolation (Friedman, 2005) can be contrasted with the concept of a "spiky" world in which intellectual capital (talent), technology infrastructure, and tolerance create magnets for growth (Florida, 2005a, 2005b). For community colleges, the world has gone from spiky to flat.

Act One: Pre-9/11, a Spiky World. Prior to September 11, 2001, globalization was largely an economic discussion, not a lived experience. International education as a concept was rooted in notions of a liberal education, not global skills or global security. For community colleges intent on meeting local needs, the level of global outreach was largely determined by the nature of the local district. Institutions that resided in districts with a culturally diverse population or global companies, or that were influenced by global economic exchange, may have developed considerable capacity for international activity. For institutions in districts that lacked these elements, however, the story was quite different. The combination of local mission and local funding exerted tremendous pressure to remain locally focused, leading to low interest by college leadership and others toward international efforts, as well as a lack of trustee board and community support for international endeavors that predictably resulted in low international student populations. Pre-9/11, the community college world was spiky, not flat, meaning that while a few community colleges were *very* internationalized, most were firmly committed to local interests.

In 2007, New Directions published *International Reform Efforts and Challenges in Community Colleges*. The editors, Rosalind Latiner Raby and Edward J. Valeau, devoted the volume to three issues: leadership; institutional development and impact of international education; and, finally, international education as a "catalyst for educational revitalization" (Raby & Valeau, 2007, p. 3). In addition to providing a historical development of international education, the volume was persuasive in making the case for international education's value; the importance of leadership, faculty, curricula, and assessment focused on international aims; and institutional approaches, such as aligning competing interests and taking an integrated approach. These issues remain relevant today; strands of continuance between Raby and Valeau's volume and our own are evident.

Act Two: Post-9/11, a Flat World.   Raby and Valeau's volume was produced with September 11, 2001, as its backdrop. As a consequence, the authors addressed the need for increasing understanding of other cultures, as well as hinting at societal fears of particular cultural groups driven by 9/11 and post-9/11 conflicts. In short, the post-9/11 context for community colleges was very different from the pre-9/11 context. Strategic interests in international engagement increased international activity in the form of development work intended to advance stability and exchange for cultural understanding. Increased participation through consortia, study-abroad opportunities, and inclusion of specific global learning outcome goals defined a post-9/11 *flattening* in which both internationalized and localized community colleges were affected by global events. Whether urban or rural, community colleges everywhere now feel the effects of globalization and are compelled to address these effects at some level.

While increased efforts to enhance international education subsequent to September 11, 2001, may have been motivated in part as a response to the event, international educational activity in recent years has been influenced by additional drivers: globalization, technology, and global demographics. In *Young World Rising*, Salkowitz (2010) warns that dramatic global population increases are unequally distributed. The developed world is aging while that of the developing world is young. Three billion of the 6.7 billion people on the planet are under 24 years old. Countries like India, Nigeria, Mexico, Brazil, Indonesia, Colombia, South Africa, the Philippines, and Vietnam are currently very young, with low per capita incomes but high technology adoption rates. These countries have the potential to gain significantly in a global economy in which traditional economic powerhouses in Europe, North America, and Japan are graying.

Salkowitz (2010) identifies and espouses a new kind of economic movement, which he refers to as "young world entrepreneurship," that is both economic and social (2010). Young world entrepreneurship is collaborative and creative, utilizing the unique blend of public, private, and nongovernmental resources available to communities and individuals. Young world entrepreneurship recognizes the economic potential of a flat world in which individual knowledge and skills can be used to find market niches in local villages or across the globe. Salkowitz sees great potential in the emergence of this young world economy, stating that "globalization unleashes talent without borders" (p. 21).

In some regions, however, the promise of economic prosperity fostered by young world entrepreneurship has been largely suppressed due to long-standing autocratic regimes, low business investment due to regional instability, and high unemployment. The Middle Eastern context, in particular, has been an area of concern due to both the inability of youth to find meaningful work and the high levels of religiosity. In many cases, the unemployed are highly educated but have received a traditional liberal arts and sciences education without employable skills. These youth lack economic agency. Armed with cell phones, Internet access, and time, legions of youth in such situations have the potential for large-scale crowdsourcing directed at simple disruption or political engagement (Herrera, 2010).

Act Three: The Post Flat World. In a post flat world, the opening of areas to trade and communications leads to conditions in which talent, technology, and tolerance become conceivable *if* an educational system like a community college is available to provide skills development. Friedman (2013) is now observing a rise of a "virtual middle class" in developing nations in which a "massive diffusion of powerful, cheap computing power via cellphones and tablets over the last decade has dramatically lowered the costs of connectivity and education—so much so that many more people in India, China and Egypt . . . now have access to the kind of technologies and learning previously associated solely with the middle class." The potential for U.S. community colleges to engage in this world has never been greater, whether in delivering programs or in advancing development of community college systems in other nations.

The community college, positioned as it is to be flexible, adaptive, open, and focused on student success, is poised to contribute across the world, but, to do so, it must engage while building capacity to advance the work for the betterment of students and communities. Inevitable forces driving globalization can allow individual talent to be leveraged through social networking for collective action or engagement independent of the geographical constraints conceptualized by Florida (2005a, 2005b). The post flat world is one in which freedom from time and distance constraints leads to new dynamics for growth and attraction of talent. Community and economic growth across a post flat world can create a new form of spiking in which local communities that fail to engage in the world lose. Providing global opportunity with local impact is thus the challenge before *all* community colleges.

References

Florida, R. (2005a). *The flight of the creative class: The new global competition for talent.* New York, NY: HarperBusiness.

Florida, R. (2005b). The world is spiky. *Atlantic Monthly, 296*(3), 48–51.

Friedman, T. (2005). *The world is flat: A brief history of the twenty-first century.* New York, NY: Farrar, Straus & Giroux.

Friedman, T. (2013, February 2). The virtual middle class rises. *New York Times.* Retrieved from http://www.nytimes.com/2013/02/03/opinion/sunday/friedman-the-virtual-middle-class-rises.html

Herrera, L. (2010). Young Egyptians' quest for jobs and justice. In L. Herrera & A. Bayat (Eds.), *Being young and Muslim* (pp. 127–143). Oxford, UK: Oxford University Press.

NEW DIRECTIONS FOR COMMUNITY COLLEGES • DOI: 10.1002/cc

Raby, R. L., & Valeau, E. J. (Eds.). (2007). *International reform efforts and challenges in community colleges.* New Directions for Community Colleges, no. 138. San Francisco, CA: Jossey-Bass.
Salkowitz, R. (2010). *Young world rising: How youth technology and entrepreneurship are changing the world from the bottom up.* Hoboken, NJ: Wiley.

TOD TREAT *is vice president for Student and Academic Services at Richland Community College in Decatur, Illinois, and adjunct assistant professor in the Department of Education Policy, Organization, and Leadership at the University of Illinois at Urbana–Champaign.*

LINDA SERRA HAGEDORN *is professor and associate dean in the College of Human Sciences at Iowa State University in Ames, Iowa.*

2

This chapter presents a model illustrating the progression of internationalization at community colleges using high-level indicators for evaluating institutional efforts in charting strategic plans for deeper global engagement.

Building Support for Internationalization Through Institutional Assessment and Leadership Engagement

Bonnie Bissonette, Shawn Woodin

Community colleges range dramatically in capacity to deliver global perspectives to students, from isolated pockets of international content to strategically leveraged global integration; however, as community college leadership recognizes the need to internationalize, the institution will progress through phases. Although the phases differ in duration and intensity due, in part, to the context of an institution, there is a distinct pattern in the evolution of internationalization. Based on observations of international efforts at more than 40 community colleges during a 4-year period, and informed by relevant research, this chapter first presents a context for understanding institutions as they pursue engagement in internationalization activities and offers specific indicators of progress so that college leaders may identify where their institution is along the spectrum. Next, we explore the framework in the context of governing board engagement because it is generally understood that board support for any college initiative is a critical factor in its success, and international education is no exception.

History of Community College Internationalization

As a national movement, community colleges have experienced four historical stages of effort of internationalization, culminating in increased recognition of the sector's global engagement. Raby and Valeau (2007) provide

NEW DIRECTIONS FOR COMMUNITY COLLEGES, no. 161, Spring 2013 © 2013 Wiley Periodicals, Inc.
Published online in Wiley Online Library (wileyonlinelibrary.com) • DOI: 10.1002/cc.20045

11

a rough time line showing that from 1967 through 1980 simple recognition began that community colleges were capable of active engagement in international education, while from 1980 to 1990 community colleges expanded and documented international activities in reaction to reports that students were not conversant with international topics. From 1990 to 2000, internationally active colleges diversified activities, including internationalizing the curriculum and proactively recruiting international students. Since 2000, community colleges have integrated global perspectives in mission statements and strategic plans (Raby & Valeau, 2007). Yet despite this progression, only a very small percentage of community colleges is highly internationalized (Green & Siaya, 2005). The same criticisms that community college students in the 1980s were internationally underinformed could very well be lodged today.

Community colleges are distinguished as the only higher education institution where internationalization is initiated either by faculty or by executive leadership at nearly equal frequency. Because community college students are less likely than their peers at other institutions to participate in education-abroad opportunities, bringing international perspectives to campus cannot be accomplished without enthusiastic and engaged faculty members. Malkan and Pisani (2011) illustrate this point and offer practical ideas to community college faculty to integrate global content in curricula as diverse as office administration, criminal justice, and computer science—all common areas of instruction at community colleges across the United States.

Institutions across higher education struggle with concepts of global competencies, and community colleges are no exception. What will international activities instill in learners? What are the anticipated learning outcomes? Clearly articulated global competencies for community college students remain nebulous. As exemplified by Mellow and Heelan (2008), "If graduates of community colleges are not *aware* [emphasis added] of global issues, and if we cannot help them to become the citizens and entrepreneurs who understand the intended and unintended consequences of out-sourcing and off-shoring, no college education will be sufficient" (p. 161). The Lumina Foundation (2011) stated that associate-level graduates should be able to "*describe* [emphasis added] how cultural perspectives could affect interpretation of problems in the arts, politics or global relations" (p. 22). Although colleges must wrestle with specific global learning outcomes for their students, the emergent trend centers on general international knowledge, not specific expertise.

In 2005, Green and Siaya reviewed data from American Council of Education's 2001 survey of all higher education institutions and distilled two groups of colleges, naming those internationally "highly active" and "less active." The resulting report suggested that highly active colleges seek external funding, have an office and a campuswide committee that solely oversee internationalization, highlight internationalization in recruitment literature, communicate internally about international opportunities, provide education abroad for credit, fund faculty professional development activities, have an international general education requirement, and fund cocurricular international activities on campus (Green & Siaya, 2005, pp. iii–iv). While providing a useful snapshot of internationalization at the time, the original study considered some factors that are not relevant for community colleges, such as research activities, and did not address critical areas such as business partnerships and continuing education. Furthermore, the report provided a suggestion of the state of internationalization at the time the survey was administered, but was not designed to describe change in capacity over time.

Following this work, Green (2012) reviewed numerous models, providing a sampling of the frameworks' shared elements, including articulated commitment, teaching and curriculum, research, budget, cocurriculum, organizational structures, education abroad, international students, faculty development, and assessment processes (pp. 7–8). In applying those models to community colleges, most dimensions are applicable, although implementation of any particular model requires translation to the context of community colleges. Specifically, the inclusion of resources directed at research activities is not pertinent to the focus of teaching and learning at most community colleges, whereas the institutional role of partnerships, workforce development, community education, and implications of open access go relatively unconsidered in other higher education models.

An additional consideration for community colleges is addressing differences between concepts of diversity and internationalization. Open access and affordability guide community college partnerships for educational solutions to shared concerns, which may be culturally distinct yet not necessarily international. For example, immigration trends over recent decades have shifted who might be considered an international student and who might be considered a domestic student within a classroom. As community colleges integrate internationalization into strategic plans, deeper ties with immigration service agencies for joint programming emerge. Engagement with immigrant populations not only enriches global diversity on campus, but it also extends the fundamental community college characteristic of open access to higher education. From the classroom perspective, a foreign student visa holder and a foreign-born U.S. permanent resident might be indistinguishable by instructors or other students.

The growing interconnectedness of cultures and their associated commingling as a result of globalization requires that educators examine the new meaning of diversity in a global context (Lim & Renshaw, 2001). The nexus between globalization's social and economic forces on higher education and recent diversity efforts highlights the strategic importance of internationalization for institutions to become welcoming and inclusive (Chun & Evans, 2009). Leadership emphasizing the local and the global enhances the educational context for students, staff, and faculty (Goddard, 2010).

Just as diversity results cannot be attained without changing the structures and day-to-day functions within an institution (Chun & Evans, 2009;
Gurin, Dey, Gurin, & Hurtado, 2003; Gurin, Dey, Hurtado, & Gurin,
2002), internationalization requires similar structural alignment. As
diversity expands to include global perspectives along with race, class,
disabilities, gender, sexual orientation, religion, and other nonmajority
perspectives, internationalization and diversity increasingly align as an
institution progresses along the spectrum.

A Model of Institutional Internationalization for Community Colleges

Colleges are highly complex and can be better understood if they are analyzed as organizations or systems (Birnbaum, 1988). This emphasizes the
dynamics of the parts within the whole, and minimizes specific individual
roles. As such, systems can be conceptualized as progressing from independent or disaggregated parts toward integrated or aggregated parts. Figure
2.1 displays institutional components that make up associated elements of
internationalization. An institution with no international capacity but with
interest would be at the disaggregated phase of the spectrum, while institutions with pervasive internationalization activities would be at the integrated side of the spectrum. The disaggregated end of the model shows a
haphazard configuration of typical college departments and resources
involved in internationalization. International development, one of the
seven elements of internationalization, does not appear at this end, repre-

Figure 2.1   Institutional Internationalization Progression

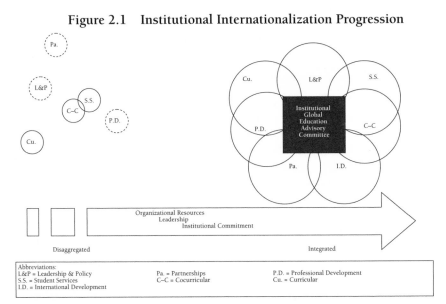

sentative that not every element would be evident at this early stage. Other elements may exist, but are displayed in dotted lines to represent the lack of institutional commitment for internationalization.

George Boggs, former president of the American Association of Community Colleges, and Judy Irwin noted that the mission, vision, and values of a college must reflect global linkages, and resources must be directed to the effort (Boggs & Irwin, 2007). Infusion of external and internal resources, leadership, and institutional commitment are represented at the bottom of Figure 2.1 inside the arrow. As institutions direct resources to internationalization, disparate elements begin to coalesce into a systematic effort.

The integrated side of Figure 2.1 displays the ideal institutional environment for comprehensive internationalization. As all departments with a role in internationalization actively engage with one another, communication crosses typical departmental lines and an institutional global education advisory committee spans the institution. The relative size of each element would vary by institution; therefore, for simplicity the model displays them with equal importance. Elements overlap in a systemic manner. Leadership and policy guide internationalization of curriculum, which is dependent on faculty and staff professional development. As college representatives create international connections through professional development activities, partnerships emerge and evolve into international development opportunities that ideally offer service learning and education-abroad experiences for students. Likewise, moving clockwise starting from leadership and policy, that element guides student services, which should closely align with cocurricular opportunities. Among internationally themed on-campus and off-campus cocurricular activities would be service learning and education-abroad efforts, which lead into international development. Moving in either direction, integrated internationalization activities create a circular, overlapping, and interdependent institutional movement.

Framework for Comprehensive Internationalization

The process of moving from disaggregated to integrated is fraught with complexities and nuances. Progression from isolated, unplanned activities to integrated, intentional, and outcomes-based strategic engagement demands institutional time and dedication, which can be conceptualized as a continuum along which internationalizing institutions can mature (Community Colleges for International Development, 2012). Community Colleges for International Development (CCID) has developed the *CCID Framework for Comprehensive Internationalization* part of CCID's overall *System of Comprehensive Internationalization* along these lines, which describes five stages beginning with no international activity to a strategically integrated institution.

Pre-Interest Phase.   Immigration trends, global competition for workers, and international flows of goods and services link all communities in a web of commerce, yet community college boards, leadership, and faculties have not actively pursued internationalization programming at some institutions. College services remain focused on local districts without acknowledgment of international ties. A standard analysis of the economic value of international import and export activities would demonstrate that local employers engage in international commerce, yet the institution is not providing students with skills necessary to engage others across borders. As individuals on a campus begin to introduce opportunities for cross-boundary awareness, the college tiptoes into the seeking phase of comprehensive internationalization.

Seeking Phase.   Scattered, disjointed, and relatively low-profile activities are hallmarks of the seeking phase. In this phase a few individual champions of internationalization may introduce global content into curricula out of personal interest or experience. Community education classes offer opportunities to interested local residents seeking a casual learning environment, such as internationally themed cooking, dancing, or conversational language. The board expresses interest in international activities, leaders begin to acknowledge the relevance of international activities, and nominal funding, if any, may support international activities. Visa-holding international students are scattered across the campus, relatively unacknowledged by college officials except as required by immigration protocols. In this phase, education-abroad experiences may not be offered for students, and internationally focused professional development may not be available to faculty members.

Building Phase.   As the college moves into the building stage, executive leaders open conversations about global competencies, among other student outcomes, and assign responsibilities for international activities within student services and academic affairs. The governance board supports investigation of internationalization at this time, and a modest budget line is approved. Mission statement revisions may include a reference to global responsibilities, and a full-time staff member coordinates disparate elements to move the institution forward.

As a college continues to build institutional internationalization capacity, education abroad emerges across multiple disciplines, and institutional policies are revised so participation in education abroad does not delay graduation for students. Institutional risk management procedures coalesce in support of outbound student mobility.

Structurally, international activities remain uncoordinated across academic units and student services departments. At one community college in the southeastern United States, this was apparent when the international education coordinator noted that neither English as a second language (ESL) faculty members nor international student advisers were represented on the college's global education committee. The existence of both, together with their absence from the committee, indicated the scattered nature of international activities of this phase at the college.

NEW DIRECTIONS FOR COMMUNITY COLLEGES • DOI: 10.1002/cc

Reaching Phase.   As an institution increases internationalization capacity, more students, staff, faculty, administrators, and trustees are aware of, engaged in, and committed to international activities. International activities mature and reach all corners of the college in this phase. Internationalization becomes more than spoken and written; it is considered in actions and decisions at all institutional levels. The governing body and executive leadership engage in global behaviors, such as hosting international groups to campus or traveling internationally as part of economic or educational delegations. Professional development activities routinely encourage global competencies for staff and faculty. The institution takes active roles in internationally focused organizations during this part of its internationalization progression.

Centralization of international activities signifies the institution's intentions to instill global awareness among all students. Financially, the institution's model balances expenditures for international activities and services with revenue sources such as grants, out-of-district tuition differential, international activities student fees, and private sector support. Internal and external communications include global themes.

Cocurricular activities featuring international topics permeate the campus. Regular events offer opportunities for partnerships between the college and the community, as well as collaboration among academic departments and student support activities. In essence, international activities begin to blur traditional silos within the college.

Innovative Phase.   Pervasive and omnipresent global perspectives touch every student, staff member, and faculty member at a comprehensively internationalized community college. An institution at this stage fully integrates internationalization in college policies, such as financial, human resources, curriculum development, risk management, and advising policies. The college's governing body promotes internationalization at the policy level while staff members at all levels, from frontline service providers to cabinet-level executives, express global perspectives.

A comprehensively internationalized college expects each student to be exposed to international content prior to graduation. Specific institutional learning outcomes articulate expectations of the global content that college employees will provide through curricular and cocurricular delivery. Academic assessments include demonstration of global competence. Technology supports and integrates internationalization.

Other indicators of fully internationalized colleges include English skills, partnerships, and international development activities. Varying English language instruction techniques such as English for academic purposes and English for speakers of other languages target foreign students and the local immigrant population. The college leaders establish clear pathways for international students to enter the U.S. higher education system through the college and to complete a bachelor's degree at another institution. Engagement in problem-solving activities in foreign countries offers learning opportunities for students at a comprehensively internationalized college.

Local Variations of the Model

What does it mean for a college to internationalize a multicampus district? Does one assess internationalization campus by campus, or for the institution overall? What is internationalization if a college's district includes a large immigrant community? How do leaders internationalize the student population if statutes preclude active foreign student recruitment? These questions are among policy-making challenges that governing boards confront during analyses of institutional internationalization, and represent place-bound nuances to a specific institution's progress along the spectrum in Figure 2.1.

Just as community colleges reflect their service districts, unlike other higher education institutions, internationalization will also mirror the community. The stages described here represent general conditions that define institutional progress; these broad descriptions are not presumed to be fully applicable at every institution. Attempting to generalize the process of systemized internationalization is limited in applicability to each local context. State statutes, governing board policies, local economic considerations, the proportion of migrant populations within service districts, and a plethora of specific institutional factors require tailoring general statements of the model to the local context.

Table 2.1 displays the numerous categories and indicators that represent potential areas of internationalization at community colleges. As internationalization progresses at an institution, progress along each indicator may be uneven. For example, a college may excel in recruiting international students and integrating them on campus, representing the integrated side of the spectrum; but its use of technology in transnational education may be offered in an isolated manner. Conversely, when state statutes preclude active recruitment of self-funded foreign students, the college may opt to apply for sponsored international students or draw visiting faculty as methods to enhance global diversity on campus.

Leadership for Internationalization

Successful international education programming at community colleges in the United States is highly dependent on meaningful support from boards of trustees; without explicit support, international education programs exist in obscurity, if they exist at all. With tacit but not explicit support from the board, international education professionals, leaders, and supporters at a community college may be able to move some programming efforts forward, but robust, multifaceted, successful international initiatives are highly unlikely. Board acknowledgment positively affects an initiative's like-

Table 2.1   Community College Internationalization
Categories and Indicators

Leadership and Policy	Organization Structure
Governance	Strategic Plan
Executive Leadership	Memberships
Mission/Core Values Committee Functions	Organization of International Activities
Policies	Finance
	Monitoring
Teaching and Learning	Internal Communication
Global Competency	External Communication
Stated Learning Outcomes	
Campus Curriculum	**Organization Personnel**
World Languages	Employee Engagement
Technology	Faculty
Continuing Education	International Programs Staff
Cocurricular	**Study Abroad**
Diversity Initiatives Campus Programs	International Travel Opportunities for
Campus Activities	Faculty/Staff
Domestic Advising	Faculty/Administration Exchanges
Delegation/Scholar Support	Health and Safety Infrastructure
	Study Abroad Academic Diversity
International Student Support	Study Abroad Geographic and Cultural
International Student Recruitment	Diversity
International Student Admissions	Student Learning During Study Abroad
International Advising	
English for Speakers of Other Languages	**Professional Development**
Domestic Articulation of International	Faculty Professional Development
Students	Workshops Faculty/Staff
International Student Integration	
	Partnerships
International Development Projects	Industry Partnerships
Student- and Faculty-Focused International	International Articulations Institutional
Development	Partnerships
Institution-Focused International	Community Partnerships Workforce
Development	Development Partnerships
Community-Focused International	
Development	

Source: Adapted from Community Colleges for International Development, 2012. Used by permission.

lihood of ending up in the general budget, which is a very strong indication of the initiative's success and longevity. Building board support requires clear, specific actions by those on campus involved and interested in international education as well as by the board members themselves.

Boards of trustees at community colleges comprise local business professionals, educational leaders, and other community members. They develop working methods and governance strategies influenced by the background and experience of individual trustees, as well as by the local setting in which the college is located. "Given the local roots and focus of community colleges, it is not surprising that institutional leaders, board members, and community members may not value global learning as much as the more immediate tasks of workforce development and teaching basic skills" (Green, 2007, p. 19). Against this backdrop, building support for international education requires the joint efforts of the board, the college president and vice presidents, and the extended college leadership team.

The makeup and operation of boards of trustees vary from college to college, as do their positions on international education initiatives. Some boards have strong philosophical support for international education, but the institution lacks facilities, staffing, or funding to move international initiatives forward. Others oversee a college with a variety of disparate international programs, occurring in isolation, with little or no communication about those initiatives to the board. Still others have formal documentation from past board actions that explicitly preclude the use of resources for international initiatives. Of course, there are some boards of trustees that have well-defined strategic plans for international education, and encourage allocation of the necessary resources to support them. Regardless of where an institution and its board are on the international education continuum, there are many steps that may be taken to develop, encourage, and grow board support for international education efforts.

Several recent publications, such as *Comprehensive Internationalization: From Concept to Action* by John K. Hudzik (2011), outline steps for higher education institutions to follow in pursuit of campus internationalization. The resources primarily address college or university leadership teams, and provide very useful guidelines for community colleges interested in building international education programming. However, the specific role of boards of trustees is not usually delineated, so here the focus is specifically on the board of trustees' leadership options and action steps to support international education.

Ultimately, a board's goal will be to establish, with college leaders, the strategic vision and plan for international education at the institution. Prior to formulating that vision, or updating an existing plan, the group will want to fully understand and assess the current international education situation (including programs, student involvement, funding, personnel, and institutional structures, among other factors).

Action Steps for Boards of Trustees and Executive Leadership

The following section describes steps for boards of trustees to take to inform themselves about international education initiatives and to grow their involvement in and support for international education.

Step One: Establish Institutional Baseline.   This is the most critical step in building support; even if a board is not initially inclined to pursue an active international education agenda, this will allow the group to understand the breadth and depth of current activities and the motivations behind them. The board should first request an assessment (report and analysis) of the international education activities and programs on campus. The assessment needs to provide all international education details, including an evaluation of institutional mission and leadership; financial and human resources; faculty role and development; curricular and extracurricular international programs and content, including study abroad; international students on campus; campus committees; community environment and sentiment; and international policies and procedures.

Step Two: Review and Discuss the Assessment. Assessment in hand, the next step for the board is to set aside an appropriate amount of time to examine and discuss the assessment and what it means. Broad stakeholder involvement is a part of asking the questions necessary to evaluate the information. The *CCID Framework for Comprehensive Internationalization* (Community Colleges for International Development, 2012) may be used as a guide for the review, or other publications that provide questions or checklists may be useful, such as *A Guide to Internationalization for Chief Academic Officers* (Hill & Green, 2008). The discussion will likely lead the board and leadership group to establish a hierarchy of sorts: programs, activities, and resources that most or all agree should be continued, followed by those programs, activities, and resources that seem to have a split opinion or need more review, and those that the majority think are unnecessary or of little value. It may be that there are board members who remain unconvinced of the value of international education and perhaps believe that all activities fall into this third category. At this juncture, it is incumbent upon the board members who see value in international education to step up and make the case if possible, asking for and using data that support the importance of international education. What items in the analysis are those that most agree should be continued or grown? It is those items that form the foundation of the strategic plan, and that even the most reticent individuals may be persuaded to support.

Step Three: Develop the Strategic Plan. As with all strategic planning, one key to success is having the right people involved in the process. The board must be involved, but also must include the right mix of allies and challengers to develop a plan that will be broadly acceptable and implementable. The plan will be specific to the college and will build on successful current programs, as well as envision new initiatives that will align with the college's mission and vision and will maximize resources. The board may take a leadership role by being actively involved in recommending a campuswide strategic planning team, having one of its members participate, if possible, and staying up to date as planning progresses. When the plan is finalized and implemented, the board and college leadership may thus all speak with one voice about the rationale for and goals of the plan. The various components of the plan are not specifically mentioned here, but it is important to note that clear and consistent communication from the board and all leaders will be critically important for successful implementation.

Step Four: Commit and Engage.   A well-communicated and well-implemented strategic plan will set international education on track for long-term success. At this point in the process, when all involved are justifiably proud of the new plan and are potentially quite tired of the meetings and planning discussions, it may be tempting for trustees to sit back and watch the plan unfold. This is exactly what they must not do. Trustees need to step up and stay involved for international education efforts to ultimately succeed. They must engage in and advocate for the approved initiatives and the resources required for those initiatives. Even trustees and boards for which the information up to this point is not new may find useful ideas for improving support and advocacy among the following actions.

A board of trustees supportive of international education is proactive, engaged, and interested as a group, and shows that support in a variety of ways. The board reviews the mission, vision, and core values of the institution for language that signals its support. If there is no mention of international or global goals, the board can make a change. It does not have to be dramatic: Highline Community College in Des Moines, Washington, clearly states the international emphasis of the institution through its mission statement on its website as of October 2012: "We deliver innovate education and training opportunities to foster your personal and professional success in our multicultural world and global economy. We help you build a better future."

A supportive board schedules an international education update at regular intervals (e.g., at each board meeting) to ensure that facets of the issue are routinely discussed and that college administration maintains accountability for international education progress. Issuing a white paper or statement about board support for international education can be a catalyst for action. For example, the board of trustees at Northcentral Technical College (NTC) in Wausau, Wisconsin, issued a white paper in 1994 in which it outlined the institution's support for international education. The paper, with the subsequent leadership of former NTC president (1993–2006) Dr. Robert Ernst and the cooperation of faculty in the residential building services program, resulted in an exchange program with a sister school in Altötting, Bavaria, which became the foundation of international education at NTC. A white paper on international education may also be used to highlight global aspects of the college for grant applications and accreditation projects.

Employee recruitment and retention, particularly for key campus leadership roles, are important areas for board involvement. Boards may consider requesting that all position descriptions include international experience as a required or desired qualification. For presidential recruitment, if a board is truly committed to international education, it will want to specifically explore candidates' global experience, if not require it. In presidential performance reviews, it is of the utmost importance to include goals related to international education to hold campus leadership account-able for implementation of the strategic plan related to international education.

Committing adequate financial resources for international education is one of the most difficult line items to maintain in a college budget, particu-larly in times of financial stress. As a result, international education is often one of the most underfunded initiatives at any institution. Boards approve the overall budget, but are not generally involved in the minutiae. One idea is for trustees to ask college leadership where international initiatives are in the general budget. Simply asking the question shows board interest and practically guarantees an answer the next time the question is asked. To make sure that funding for international education is reliable, boards need to be sure that strategic planning includes specific outcomes to which funds may be linked. Defending expenditures on international education may be easier for all if stated in terms of student learning outcomes. If creating global citizens is one of the institution's stated goals, then aligning funding with the activities needed to reach that goal may make sense to most stake-holders. An important comparison for the board to request is that of income generated by international education (international student tuition and fees, education abroad fees, grants, or program funding) to funds spent on international education. The difference may not be as perceived, and the balance may provide a strong defense for funding.

Individual trustees can do much to support and advance international education, in addition to being actively involved in the board as group members. They may attend international events on campus and in the com-munity, offer to mentor an international student or be a conversation part-ner with an ESL student, or attend conferences or sessions at conferences that address international education. The Association of Community College Trustees had an intentional series of sessions devoted to internatio-nal education best practices at the 2009 Congress in San Francisco. Board members attending such conferences would do well to seek out those ses-sions that include new ideas and innovations.

Are international students hosting an informational talk about a speci-fic region of the world? Is the entrepreneurship class traveling to Brazil for a 1-week exploration of small business incubation in São Paulo? Trustees can attend or join in a group to not only show support, but also learn more about the international activities of the college. Joining a student group as a trustee is particularly effective if the trustee is familiar with the country to which the group is traveling and can share experiences.

Supporting international education in the broader community is a critically important role for trustees and one that individual members of the board need to consciously resolve to play. Encouraging development of an internationalized mind-set in the community means being there and

showing commitment. When community members comment on outsour-
cing of jobs, trustees must speak up to talk about ways the college is training students to compete in the global economy. Familiarity with academic
offerings of all kinds is important for a trustee, and internationalized curricula in particular can benefit from board knowledge and support.

An Engaged and Supportive Board.   What does an engaged and
supportive board look like? Painting a picture using the previous recommendations and drawing directly from the descriptors of an "innovative
board" on the *CCID Framework for Comprehensive Internationalization*
(Community Colleges for International Development, 2012), it is clear. An
engaged and supportive board "advocates for international activities;
expects and demands accountability to international goals; specifies international education in a multilayered way; establishes a high level college
international education committee and empowers it to make decisions
about international activities; integrates international education into college policies, with a process of regular review; and includes international
strategic priorities in annual plans at all levels."

Summary

Community colleges, by their nature, focus on the skills of the local population within designated service districts. Increasingly, as globalization per-
meates even the smallest businesses and communities, global competencies
are demanded by employers. The ability to understand and effectively interact with people of diverse backgrounds and cultures grows increasingly
common among expected workforce skills. Community colleges vary con-
siderably in how they meet demands by businesses for workers with global
competencies. The college should seek to define what global competencies
are expected of students as a result of internationalization, and then define
a strategy within its context.

No matter where a board starts, the important thing is that it takes
action to move forward. "Though enthusiasm for a given program or initiative is never universal on any campus, widespread faculty and administrative
leadership is essential in creating institutional energy, imparting legitimacy,
and achieving broad participation" (Green, 2007, p. 22). International education at community colleges is a growing focus in the United States, and
boards of trustees are important decision makers in the leadership negotia-
tion about the relative priority of international education. Building board
support is accomplished by college leadership partnering with the board,
providing extensive data, and evaluating the current international education
situation, openly and in great detail. Once the board has a clear understanding of the present, it may look to the future.

Is the integration of internationalization an end in itself? No.
Comprehensive internationalization is a process without an end point. As
community colleges continue to evolve and address the needs of how their

local communities interact with global economic flows, and as local workers compete for jobs with workers in faraway lands, strategies of internationalization will progress in exciting, unknowable trajectories. A comprehensively internationalized institution with unwavering board support will be strategically poised to adapt to future global shifts.

References

Birnbaum, R. (1988). *How colleges work: The cybernetics of academic organization and leadership.* San Francisco, CA: Jossey-Bass.
Boggs, G. R., & Irwin, J. (2007). What every community college leader needs to know: Building leadership for international education. In R. L. Raby & E. J. Valeau (Eds.), *International reform efforts and challenges in community colleges* (pp. 25–30). New Directions for Community Colleges, no. 138. San Francisco, CA: Jossey-Bass.
Chun, E., & Evans, A. (2009). Bridging the diversity divide: Globalization and reciprocal empowerment in higher education. *ASHE Higher Education Report, 35*(1), 1–142.
Community Colleges for International Development. (2012). *CCID system of comprehensive internationalization.* Retrieved from https://programs.ccid.cc/cci/
Goddard, J. (2010). Toward glocality: Facilitating leadership in an age of diversity. *Journal of School Leadership, 20*(1), 37–56.
Green, M. F. (2007). Internationalizing community colleges: Barriers and strategies. In R. L. Raby & E. J. Valeau (Eds.), *International reform efforts and challenges in community colleges* (pp. 15–24). New Directions for Community Colleges, no. 138. San Francisco, CA: Jossey-Bass.
Green, M. F. (2012). *Measuring and assessing internationalization.* Washington, DC: NAFSA: Association of International Educators. Retrieved from http://www.nafsa.org/resourcelibrary/Default.aspx?id=32455
Green, M., & Siaya, L. (2005). Measuring internationalization at community colleges. Washington, DC: American Council on Education. Retrieved from http://www.acenet.edu/news-room/Pages/Measuring-Internationalization-Community-Colleges.aspx
Gurin, P., Dey, E. L., Gurin, G., & Hurtado, S. (2003). How does racial/ethnic diversity promote education? *Western Journal of Black Studies, 27,* 20–29.
Gurin, P., Dey, E. L., Hurtado, S., & Gurin, G. (2002). Diversity and higher education: Theory and impact on educational outcomes. *Harvard Educational Review, 72*(3), 330–336.
Hill, B., & Green, M. (2008). *A guide to internationalization for chief academic officers.* Washington, DC: American Council on Education.
Hudzik, J. (2011). *Comprehensive internationalization: From concept to action.* Washington, DC: NAFSA: Association of International Educators.
Lim, L., & Renshaw, P. (2001). The relevance of sociocultural theory to culturally diverse partnerships and communities. *Journal of Child and Family Studies, 10*(1), 9–21.
Lumina Foundation. (2011). The degree qualifications profile. Retrieved from http://www.luminafoundation.org/publications/The_Degree_Qualifications_Profile.pdf
Malkan, R., & Pisani, M. (2011). Internationalizing the community college experience. *Community College Journal of Research and Practice, 35*(11), 825–841.
Mellow, G. O., & Heelan, C. (2008). *Minding the dream: The process and practice of the American community college.* Lanham, MD: Rowman & Littlefield.
Raby, R. L., & Valeau, E. J. (2007). Community college international education: Looking back to forecast the future. In R. L. Raby & E. J. Valeau (Eds.), *International reform efforts and challenges in community colleges* (pp. 5–14). New Directions for Community Colleges, no. 138. San Francisco, CA: Jossey-Bass.

BONNIE BISSONETTE is the associate director of the Student Center for Global Education at the University of Maryland, Baltimore, and spent more than 9 years leading international education efforts at Northcentral Technical College, Wausau, Wisconsin.

SHAWN WOODIN is the national director of the U.S. Department of State–funded Community College Initiative at Community Colleges for International Development, Inc., and has worked with internationalization efforts at 43 community colleges from Cape Cod to Honolulu.

NEW DIRECTIONS FOR COMMUNITY COLLEGES • DOI: 10.1002/cc

3

This chapter describes how the American higher education system is about to witness unprecedented growth in the number of foreign students studying on U.S. campuses. Presidents and governing board members are challenged to leverage this threshold moment to achieve comprehensive internationalization.

International Students as a Resource for Achieving Comprehensive Internationalization

Michael Brennan, Donald A. Dellow

Defining Comprehensive Internationalization

Jane Knight is most often credited with establishing the term *internationalization* as a process in higher education. Her seminal works in the 1990s established internationalization not as a state to be achieved, but as an ongoing process by which colleges could strive to increase the global learning of students (Knight, 1993, 1994).

Building on the work of Knight and others, the American Council on Education (ACE) published a series of working papers on internationalization of higher education that helped to frame much of the dialogue and strategy for internationalization of higher education in the United States (Engleberg & Green, 2002; Green, 2005; Green & Olson, 2003; Green & Shoenberg, 2006; Hayward & Siaya, 2001; Olson, Green, & Hill, 2005, 2006). In *A Handbook for Advancing Comprehensive Internationalization* (Olson, Green, & Hill, 2006), the ACE authors establish a case for global education and define a framework for "comprehensive internationalization." They define global learning as the "knowledge, skills, and attitudes that enable students to understand world cultures and events; analyze global systems; appreciate cultural differences; and apply this knowledge and appreciation to their lives as citizens and workers" (p. v). To achieve

NEW DIRECTIONS FOR COMMUNITY COLLEGES, no. 161, Spring 2013 © 2013 Wiley Periodicals, Inc.
Published online in Wiley Online Library (wileyonlinelibrary.com) • DOI: 10.1002/cc.20046

integration of such global learning, Olson, Green, and Hill (2006) argue for comprehensive internationalization that stresses the synergy that can be achieved when internationalization activities, including study abroad, international students, and a globalized curriculum, are integrated within a coherent and holistic framework of internationalization goals and measures:

> Institutions working to advance comprehensive internationalization articulate internationalization as an institutional goal, develop internationalization plans based on an analysis of current efforts, and seek to make the whole greater than the sum of its parts by creating synergy among diverse internationalization initiatives across the institution. (p. vii)

In another influential working paper in the ACE series, *Where Faculty Live: Internationalizing the Disciplines,* Madeline Green and Robert Shoenberg make a compelling case that internationalization cannot be relegated to key courses or only to study-abroad programs, but rather that "infusing international, global, and intercultural perspectives across courses and programs . . . is the key strategy to ensure that *all* students learn about other nations, languages, cultures, and histories, and global issues" (2006, p. 1). Green and Shoenberg argue compellingly that, with the growing importance of global competency in all fields of study, it is critical to find ways to integrate international education into all disciplines, and, to do so, institutions will need to engage and inspire faculty who can make global learning relevant to disciplinary content in the classroom.

Given the growing recognition that global competency is a crucial element for higher education to address at all levels, it is somewhat surprising that community colleges continue to wrestle with including elements of international work as a central educational goal. As addressed elsewhere in this volume, boards of trustees' lack of knowledge about globalization, a lack of consistent executive leadership, a lack of commitment from faculty, and the impact of funding formulas' emphasis on local sources can all contribute to a sense that international work is beyond the mission of community colleges.

Despite the aforementioned challenges, there is subtle evidence that community colleges are becoming more open to internationalization. A survey of the landscape reveals that colleges are becoming more engaged in international endeavors. For example, attendance is growing each year at the annual conferences organized by international education associations. Researchers and others are writing more about community college internationalization, and increasingly doctoral students are addressing the topic in their dissertations. Nevertheless, the empirical evidence indicates that progress toward internationalization has been slow. Each of the authors of this chapter brings over 20 years of experience advocating for the internationalization of community colleges. We are therefore encouraged, as we believe we are on the verge of a viral acceleration of comprehensive internationalization among community colleges. Author Malcolm Gladwell would describe this moment as a "tipping point," which is "that magic moment when an idea, trend, or social behavior crosses a threshold, tips, and spreads like wildfire" (Gladwell, 2002, p. 12). Employing his insights, we believe big changes are about to follow decades of incremental progress. Governing board members, college presidents, and faculty dedicated to connecting their campuses to the world will pivot to take advantage of this threshold moment. Others, more content with the gradualist approach, may miss out.

A National Call to Action

As a "conscious effort to integrate and infuse international, intercultural, and global dimensions into the ethos and outcomes of postsecondary education" (NAFSA, 2012), internationalization requires more than enrolling international students, sending a few students abroad, or organizing the occasional international cultural event. It requires that everyone involved in the education of students work to build a learning environment that prepares students for a global society. For this to occur, administrative teams must be committed to making their campuses more globally aware and committed to change. Two of the most fundamental aspects of effective leadership in any situation are that leaders "model the way" and create a "shared vision" (Kouzes & Posner, 2007). Community college leadership teams, starting with boards of trustees and presidents, must be knowledgeable about how globalization is changing the world and their communities.

The two national organizations that guide the community college movement, the American Association of Community Colleges (AACC) and the Association of Community College Trustees (ACCT), issued a joint statement (AACC/ACCT, 2006) on the role of community colleges in international education, stating that "community colleges should develop strategic plans for global awareness and competence that respond to the needs of the community's learners, businesses, and institutions." The directive is clearly established at the national level, and it is up to presidents and senior college officials to implement strategic plans and promote greater global awareness at the local, campus level.

Presidents leading the internationalization of their institutions take every opportunity to encourage students to think more globally, challenge faculty to reconsider their curricula from a global perspective, and work to secure funding for internationalization initiatives. As Kotter (1996) notes, a vision, such as promoting greater global awareness and action, must be reaffirmed repeatedly over time. In our view, community colleges that have acted to internationalize will see their efforts rewarded, provided that they discern we are approaching a threshold moment and align their capabilities to exploit it.

NEW DIRECTIONS FOR COMMUNITY COLLEGES • DOI: 10.1002/cc

The Competitive Advantage: The President, Plan, and Chief International Officer

In 2005 the American Association of Community Colleges published a list of leadership competencies considered important for the effective leadership of community college presidents. The document included 45 specific competencies, with six being core. One of the 45 specific competencies was: "Demonstrate cultural competence in a global society." Although cultural competence is not a sine qua non for a global view, it is a major goal for any effort to create a more global perspective on campus.

ACE offers a Survey of Internationalization that in 2011 polled 239 community colleges on key benchmarks of internationalization. Unfortunately, that number was lower than the number surveyed in 2006. When the results of the 2011 survey (reported in American Council on Education, 2012) were compared to the 2006 survey, there was a modest increase in the prevalence of key indicators of internationalization on community college campuses, but on most indicators fewer than 25% of respondent 2-year colleges reported having an internationalization plan.

One of the interesting findings of the 2011 survey was that the president was described as the most "vital catalyst" in promoting internationalization. Understandably, community college presidents play a pivotal role in setting the stage for other campus advocates. A president who invests in a full-time chief international officer (CIO), for example, understands the complexities of advancing the international agenda and recognizes the value of capacity building for the purpose of leading change. We would argue that institutions guided by thoughtful internationalization plans that are mandated by presidents and executed by a CIO enjoy competitive advantages over their sister institutions; they are in a stronger position to leverage the change that is fast approaching. They will become the innovators that others will follow.

The Tipping Point. In the context of decreasing government funding for U.S. higher education and a corresponding growing dependence on student tuition and fees when shaping annual budgets, the potential exists to gain a reliable funding stream from increased international enrollments, which do not presume state subsidy. We are witnessing an extraordinary opportunity for international education. We are standing at the threshold between a time when we expected incremental internationalization and a new frontier of high-speed change that will be optimized only by colleges at the ready. The leadership exerted by Community Colleges for International Development (CCID), AACC, and ACCT petitioning presidents and governing board members to plan strategically for global awareness and competence will continue to be critical in this new era, especially for the colleges that have not heeded the call to build the capacity required for navigating the complexities and opportunities moving forward. It is our

NEW DIRECTIONS FOR COMMUNITY COLLEGES • DOI: 10.1002/cc

view that demand for U.S. higher education and the means to provide foreign students unprecedented access to it are converging. The result will be a geometric progression of the number of international students in the American higher education system. Community colleges that successfully harness this tipping point will comprehensively internationalize their institutions for the benefit of their students and communities.

In the aftermath of the recent economic downturn, many existing entities are expanding and new organizations are emerging to capitalize on the revenue stream represented by international students studying at U.S. colleges and universities. NAFSA conservatively estimates that international students and their dependents made a $21.81 billion contribution to the U.S. economy during the 2011–2012 academic year. Institutions of higher education are driving the fast-forward movement of recruiting international students to the United States.

In a manner consistent with its mission of encouraging mutual understanding among nations, the U.S. Department of State is expanding efforts to promote U.S. higher education to prospective international students through the new Education USA brand for overseas advising offices. Education USA is a global network of hundreds of advising centers supported by the Bureau of Educational and Cultural Affairs at the U.S. Department of State.

In May 2011, Hillsborough Community College, the University of Tampa, the University of South Florida, and the Institute of International Education (IIE) worked collaboratively to design and deliver the first of a planned new series of professional development workshops for Education USA advisers. The training modules were built with a focus on the American higher education system with specific emphasis on the participating schools' three distinct campus cultures—public university, private university, and community college—and the international student experience. The effort produced a training manual to provide exercises, lecture material, and suggestions for reflection. The IIE continues to solicit proposals from U.S. institutions for similar training workshops, including programs designed to go beyond the basics for advisers. Community colleges determined to gain more expertise in the field and expand their relationships with universities to include cooperation on international student programming would be well advised to join forces to host future Education USA workshops.

Beginning in June 2010, the State Department began organizing the Education USA Forum in the nation's capital. The event brings together Education USA advisers, regional education advising coordinators, State Department officials, embassy officials, and representatives from colleges and universities actively involved in international student programming. During the third annual Education USA Forum, for example, sessions on regional trends and developments, including insights into countries underrepresented on U.S. campuses but with growing promise for colleges willing to be among the first to visit for recruiting purposes, were in such demand they were standing room only.

Adopting a more businesslike approach, the U.S. Department of Commerce is expanding education trade missions and Gold Key (GK) services in the education sector. In April 2011, for example, Undersecretary Francisco Sanchez led an education trade mission of U.S. colleges and universities to Indonesia and Vietnam. The U.S. Commercial Service (international arm of the Commerce Department) is increasingly present at international education conferences to sell its services to colleges interested in developing business relationships in nations around the world. The GK service can also link colleges with vetted student recruitment agencies.

Perhaps the most unambiguous sign that recruiting international students is fast becoming an integral part of enrollment management plans and comprehensive internationalization at U.S. higher education institutions is the emergence of the American International Recruitment Council (AIRC) in 2008, an association dedicated to helping accredited U.S. postsecondary institutions and student recruitment agencies collaborate on agreed-upon quality standards for international student placement. AIRC is a standards development organization that follows global practice for quality assurance processes to certify recruiting agencies meeting AIRC standards. As described in its marketing materials, "for the purposes of AIRC membership and certification, an agency is defined as an organization, company or association that recruits and places students into accredited colleges, universities and other educational institutions on a commercial 'fee for service' basis."

Regardless of philosophical stand on the issue of engaging the services of overseas agencies to recruit international students, AIRC's rapid development, as reflected in the growing number of higher education institutions becoming members, is another significant measure of the accelerated pace of change in the field.

Of the 17 current community college members of AIRC, only two are among the top tier of associate degree institutions hosting international students (see later discussion). In other words, 15 community colleges, perhaps determined to join their sister institutions at the top, are investing in their capacity to grow international enrollments.

A select group of institutions, located for the most part on the nation's West Coast or in major metropolitan areas, are leaders among community colleges in international student programming. Either out of necessity because their location naturally attracts foreign students or as a result of a deliberate plan, these colleges have the experience to manage the rapid change and maximize the corresponding opportunities that are approaching. According to the 2012 Institute of International Education *Open Doors Report*, associate degree institutions belonging to the "top 40" educated a total of 48,552 international students in the 2011–2012 academic year. The total number of international students attending U.S. community colleges in the same year was 87,977, or 1.1% of total community college enrollments. These enrollments represent a 2.1% decline from the previous year.

The question facing the 1,092 community colleges not among the top 40[1] is: Does your institution have the presidential leadership, strategic plan, and CIO to optimize both the bottom-line financial benefits and the multiplier effect that many will derive from the forthcoming exponential growth in international student numbers? The question that community colleges as a group must confront is: Do they want to leverage competitive advantages to secure a greater market share, or are they ready to yield the benefits of the rapid changes ahead to 4-year colleges and universities? As documented in the 2012 *Open Doors Report*, a record-high 764,495 international students—an increase of 5.7% over the previous year—studied in the United States. Clearly, community colleges lag behind.

While the demand around the world for U.S. higher education is growing and more players are expanding access to it, international students have choices. Institutions wanting to differentiate themselves from the competition will soon learn that international students choose one college over another for many reasons, including whether the learning environment respects cultural differences. If domestic students attending community colleges lack critical thinking skills, an awareness of other cultures, and an understanding that their own cultural perspectives influence their understanding of different cultures, growing international student enrollments will be a difficult task.

Money Matters.   Executing plans aimed at increasing international (F-1 visa) enrollments and expanding international learning opportunities requires consensus on a long-term resource allocation model. Although specific financial arrangements are dependent on the particular circumstances of each campus, community colleges currently enjoying robust F-1 student revenues share the following two practices:

1. Quality academic and support services for F-1 students that grow as student numbers increase.
2. Commitment to a revenue-sharing formula that yields a return for the college *and* international education.

A revenue allocation model that delivers a financial return to the college and deliberately places international education on a cost-recovery, entrepreneurial path facilitates growing F-1 student enrollments and investing in multiplier effect initiatives. In other words, over the longer term, the college supports a series of integrated initiatives to nurture a learning environment that prepares students for an increasingly interconnected and changing world. Internationalization becomes part of the ethos or culture of the institution.

If a community college currently educates even a small number of international (F-1 visa) students, strategically realigning existing F-1 student revenues to deliver quality services is a responsible and ethical first step toward accelerating F-1 revenue growth. For example, one of the authors determined that an F-1 student taking 30 credit hours in pursuit of an associate of arts degree at his institution generated 13 times more net gain revenue than a resident student.

In the near term, expanding international student enrollments and taking steps toward comprehensive internationalization produce many benefits beyond the much-needed nonresident tuition revenues. Depending on the varied circumstances at a particular institution, immediate outcomes may include:

- Developing the capacity to provide programs and services to international students *and* internationally minded U.S. students.
- Bringing global perspectives into the classroom for the benefit of all students.
- Achieving retention and completion rates exceeding the state average.
- Establishing or leveraging existing English as a second language instructional capacity to increase international enrollments and deliver revenue-generating summer programs.
- Sustaining faculty professional development, including workshops focused on optimizing cultural diversity in the classroom and communicating across cultures.

The Talent Search. In his executive summary for the recent NAFSA report, *Comprehensive Internationalization: From Concept to Action*, John K. Hudzik emphasizes that building a coherent institutional approach to internationalization requires "leadership (a) that is senior and influential enough to promote development of an institutional consensus and strategy . . . and (b) that can help facilitate development of synergies across the programming components of internationalization" (Hudzik, 2011, p. 3).

Too often, community colleges designate a campus president, vice president, dean, or faculty member to manage international education instead of installing a full-time and fully qualified CIO. When the responsibility for promoting internationalization is a shared responsibility or an add-on responsibility, there is a likelihood that it will not receive the attention it needs and deserves.

Suffice it to say that a capable CIO is responsible for the drumbeat guiding internationalization efforts. Determining the pace and rhythm of progress requires putting together a thoughtful, intentional strategic plan with input from a wide range of stakeholders. Executing the plan and achieving desired outcomes require reaching consensus on a funding formula and then steadfastly defending the same. Additionally, the most important advocacy role the CIO must play is to insist on recruiting and investing in the professional development of exceptionally qualified staff for the purpose of optimizing the internationalization process and nurturing future leaders. A team of professionals who have lived in other countries for a sustained period of time as Peace Corps volunteers, English teachers, or grassroots development officers and who speak one or more foreign languages brings credibility to the internationalization effort, particularly when engaging faculty in programming to promote greater awareness and action on behalf of domestic students.

The CIO will identify, cultivate, and maintain effective partnerships across campus and abroad to promote international education, faculty and student exchanges, and curriculum initiatives. The CIO will manage a range of international programs, partnerships, and initiatives on campus and around the world.

Learning the international student recruitment landscape, aligning internal business processes to support working with international constituencies, disseminating information on progress, and advocating to college leaders the importance of persistence and patience all require the coordination and leadership of a full-time, dedicated CIO. A sustained effort by the CIO and other professionals is required when ensuring the delivery of support programming to students, generating brand recognition in different cultures, and building relationships with organizations and individuals, including students and their parents, in other countries.

Exploit the Plus Two.   The strengths of the community college, including price point, small class sizes, and dedicated faculty and staff support, do not always translate when trying to recruit prospective international students, because many prospective students do not understand the community college concept. In many nations, a community college equivalent does not exist. Several pioneering community colleges, including many in the top 40, have turned this weakness into an opportunity. They have exploited the "plus two" of the 2 + 2 equation. In other words, they have successfully branded their campuses as gateways to highly regarded 4-year institutions.

Over a sustained period of time, dedicated, campus-based advisers have defined with precision which courses an international student should take to gain acceptance into his or her choice of university, and increasingly they are mapping the way into a specific college or program within the preferred university. As a result, the CIO and recruitment staff meeting prospective students and their parents at college fairs and high schools around the world can highlight success stories of former students who earned their bachelor's degrees from selective liberal arts colleges, nationally ranked research universities, and Ivy League institutions. Community colleges launching efforts to grow international student enrollments should be mindful of the progress made by sister colleges, particularly in several Asian markets, positioning community colleges as an alternative freshman sophomore pathway to a highly regarded 4-year bachelor's degree.

NEW DIRECTIONS FOR COMMUNITY COLLEGES • DOI: 10.1002/cc

Creating a Culture of Evidence

Any effort to internationalize must be intentional and executed in the context of a community college's core values and academic strengths. In addition to the benefits offered by the organizations listed earlier for student recruitment, resources are available to support planning and measuring the impact of comprehensive international programming. CCID has developed, for example, a *System of Comprehensive Internationalization* (Community Colleges for International Development, 2012)—a tool specifically for community colleges embarking or already on a path to increasing "the level and quality of activity in international education and measuring progress in the form of metrics."

Final Thoughts

Many community colleges have readily moved toward recruiting and enrolling international students, encouraged in part by the double or triple tuition these students pay, which adds to the bottom line of the general operating fund. The increased reliance by U.S. higher education institutions on student tuition and fees to fund operations will only increase the number of institutions exploring the alternative revenue stream international students represent. The purpose of this chapter was to underscore the importance of presidential leadership, a thoughtful plan, and a capable CIO to maximize the opportunities that will surely result from the fast-approaching tipping point. Just as U.S. institutions are increasing their footprint in the international student recruitment sector, we are witnessing a growing demand for U.S. higher education around the world, and a flurry of activity by several different organizations—new and old—to meet this demand. We believe that community colleges need to hit the reset button. Years of slow, incremental progress in internationalization have lulled many community college educators into a gradualist mentality. Community colleges need to embrace a new sense of urgency. It is not as easy to recruit and retain international students as just deciding to do so, like turning on a switch. To succeed, the effort must be undertaken thoughtfully and with a stubborn commitment to bringing the world home to our domestic students, internationalizing our colleges comprehensively. Is your institution ready to maximize a return from the tipping point, or will you be left behind?

Note

1. AACC's 2012 *Community College Fact Sheet* reports that there are 1,132 community colleges in the United States.

References

AACC/ACCT joint statement on the role of community colleges in international education. (2006). Retrieved from http://www.aacc.nche.edu/About/Positions/Pages/ps10012006. aspx

American Association of Community Colleges. (2005). *Competencies for community college leaders.* Retrieved from http://www.ccleadership.org/resourcecenter/competencies.htm

American Council on Education. (2012). *Mapping internationalization on U.S. campuses: 2012 edition.* Retrieved from http://www.acenet.edu/news-room/Documents/MappingInternationalizationonUSCampuses2012-full.pdf

American International Recruitment Council. (2008). Retrieved from http://www.airc-education.org/about-airc

Community Colleges for International Development. (2012). *CCID system of comprehensive internationalization.* Retrieved from https://programs.ccid.cc/cci/sites/default/files/images/SCI_Exec_FCI%201.1_Userguide.pdf

Engleberg, D., & M. F. Green. (2002). *Promising practices: Spotlighting excellence in comprehensive internationalization.* Washington, DC: American Council on Education.

Gladwell, M. (2002). *The tipping point: How little things can make a big difference.* New York, NY: Back Bay Books.

Green, M. F. (2005). *Internationalization in U.S. higher education: The student perspective.* Washington, DC: American Council on Education.

Green, M. F., & C. Olson. (2003). *Internationalizing the campus: A user's guide.* Washington, DC: American Council on Education.

Green, M., & R. Shoenberg. (2006). *Where faculty live: internationalizing the disciplines.* Washington, DC: American Council on Education.

Hayward , F., & L. Siaya. (2001). *Report on two surveys about internationalization.* Washington, DC: American Council of Education.

Hudzik, J. K. (2011). *Comprehensive internationalization: From concept to action (executive summary).* Washington, DC: NAFSA. Retrieved from http://www.nafsa.org/uploadedFiles/NAFSA_Home/Resource_Library_Assets/Publications_Library/2011_Comprehen_Internationalization.pdf

Institute of International Education. (2012). *Open Doors report.* Retrieved on January 14, 2013, from http://www.iie.org/Research-and-Publications/Open-Doors/Data/Special-Reports/Community-College-Data-Resource/International-Students-Top-Host-Institutions-2011-12

Knight, J. (1993). Internationalization: Management strategies and issues. *International Education, 2,* 21–22.

Knight, J. (1994). Checkpoints for an internationalization strategy. *CBIE Research,* no. 7.

Kotter, J. P. (1996). *Leading change.* Boston, MA: Harvard Business School Press.

Kouzes, J. M., & Posner, B. Z. (2007). *Leadership challenge.* San Francisco, CA: Jossey-Bass.

NAFSA. (2012). The changing landscape of higher education. Retrieved from http://www.nafsa.org/_/File/_/positioning_brochure.pdf

Olson, C. L., Green, M. F., & Hill, B. A. (2005). *Building a strategic framework for comprehensive internationalization.* Washington, DC: American Council on Education.

Olson, C. L., Green, M. F., & Hill, B. A. (2006). *A handbook for advancing comprehensive internationalization: What institutions can do and what students should learn.* Washington, DC: American Council on Education.

MICHAEL BRENNAN *is the director of International Education at Hillsborough Community College in Tampa, Florida.*

DONALD A. DELLOW *is associate professor of Higher Education at the University of South Florida in Tampa, Florida.*

4

This chapter examines faculty-led study-abroad programs as a strategy for increasing the breadth and depth of internationalization in community college education and uses the case study of Madison Area Technical College to examine the role of comprehensive internationalization in community college education.

Internationalization and Faculty-Led Service Learning

Geoffrey W. Bradshaw

In 2010, Madison Area Technical College (Madison College), a comprehensive community college in Madison, Wisconsin, was selected by the U.S. Department of State, Bureau of Education and Cultural Affairs (ECA) to head a consortium project to expand the capacity of community colleges to offer study-abroad programs. The project focuses on strengthening the capacity of colleges to offer study abroad and on developing service learning programs related to renewable energy, engineering, and sustainable development in Central America and the Caribbean. Madison College has used this award to create the Community College Sustainable Development Network (CCSDN), a consortium of 24 community colleges working collaboratively to develop new faculty-led study-abroad opportunities, and an experiential education training program that shares best practices in new study-abroad program development. This chapter uses examples from the Madison College experience and lessons from the CCSDN model to illustrate best practices in community college internationalization.

Community College Internationalization

"Transforming lives, one at a time" happens to be the institutional tag line for Madison College. But for those of us working in the field of international education, there is no phrase more apt to capture the aspirations of

New Directions for Community Colleges, no. 161, Spring 2013 © 2013 Wiley Periodicals, Inc.
Published online in Wiley Online Library (wileyonlinelibrary.com) • DOI: 10.1002/cc.20047

student exchange and intercultural learning. With a few notable excep-
tions, however, community colleges have been historically slow to integrate
international education into the core of their mission. For most community
colleges, *community* has been defined not in global terms, but very clearly
as the tax district or catchment area for local enrollment. The mission of
community colleges has been to educate the local population in job skills
for employment in local industry or help them get into a state college to
continue a 4-year or other advanced degree.

In the former era of agricultural and industrial economies, there was
no need for community colleges to spend significant time or energy on
international issues. If the goal was to prepare students for employment
within the district in jobs that had little or no global engagement, then
international education was logically seen as extraneous to the core mission
of community colleges—something nice to have, but not essential.

In that same era, those engaged in the community college transfer mission often assumed that international issues could be addressed by 4-year
colleges in the advanced stages of a bachelor's degree. The role of community colleges was to provide students with a basic skills foundation of general education courses, and if students were interested in international
issues, they could choose to specialize in fields such as world history,
anthropology, or political science later in their academic careers after transferring to a 4-year college or university.

Study abroad was even less likely to be historically integrated into
community college programs. For many, if not most, Americans, study
abroad was seen as a luxury for wealthy students who might travel as part
of a junior year abroad. Study abroad was generally seen as part of the
humanities, world languages study, or specific disciplines such as anthropology or international relations.

Today, however, we live in a world in which economic, political, and
environmental issues of our age are all inextricably linked to global forces
and trends. Contemporary employers are demanding that students know
how to work with diverse teams, supply chains, and customer networks
that span multiple international borders. Community college graduates are
now expected to be prepared to communicate with people from all over the
world and to understand complex global economic changes, and they are
told to expect even greater global integration throughout the course of their
lifetimes.

For community college students who are transferring to 4-year colleges and universities, it is no longer appropriate to assume that general
education courses devoid of international content will be sufficient to prepare them with a strong foundation for academic success. Rather, students
are expected to come into 4-year programs with a strong foundation of
global literacy upon which to build greater knowledge and specialization.
Today it is not just students majoring in disciplines such as world history,
anthropology, and political science who must have a foundation of global

literacy; rather, nearly every field of study is in the process of integrating global competencies that will allow students to solve problems and work effectively in today's globally integrated world.

The era in which education abroad was only a luxury for wealthy juniors at large universities and elite private schools is also long past. Today we have a responsibility to provide students with the opportunity to engage in transformative experiential learning programs where they can build their global competencies through firsthand experience at all institutions of higher learning.

The extent to which these changes in the importance of study abroad and global competency in higher education have shifted is reflected in the way that national leaders increasing articulate these issues as part of public discourse. First Lady Michelle Obama, for example, highlighted the importance of global job skills and the need for increased study abroad in an address at Howard University in 2011:

> Studying abroad isn't just an important part of a well-rounded educational experience. It's also becoming increasingly important for success in the modern global economy. Getting ahead in today's workplaces isn't just about the skills you bring from the classroom. It's also about the experience you have with the world beyond our borders—with people, and languages, and cultures that are very different from our own. (Quoted by Mulholland, 2011)

The First Lady's remarks were part of the announcement of a 100,000 Strong initiative aimed at having 100,000 Americans study in China over 4 years, which was followed by a similar initiative to foster connections in Latin America with particular emphasis on new partnerships with Brazil. Key to the 100,000 Strong initiative is a call for increased participation of community college students and other underrepresented populations in study-abroad programs.

National dialogue on internationalization and increasing capacity for study abroad has increasingly called for greater engagement of community college students in education-abroad initiatives. In 2005 a congressionally authorized Blue Ribbon Commission was appointed to establish recommendations for increasing the numbers of U.S. students participating in study abroad to reach a goal of a million study-abroad students within 10 years. The resulting report, *Global Competence and National Needs: One Million Americans Studying Abroad*, specifically calls for programs that expand access to study abroad at community colleges:

> Access to the campus has been one of the great successes of American higher education. In the emerging world, equal access to study abroad must become an institutional and national priority. Study abroad should no longer be largely the domain of students from large research universities and small, selective, liberal arts colleges. (2005, pp. 27–28)

Internationalization at Madison College

The evolution of international programs at Madison College has largely mirrored the larger arc of community college internationalization. Prior to the mid-1990s, the college had no formal international initiatives aside from a few isolated faculty in the humanities who had pioneered some early noncredit educational travel tours to Europe. Diversity initiatives at the college were defined almost entirely in terms of domestic race and ethnicity, and such efforts drew their impetus more from civil rights struggles for multicultural inclusivity in campus life and the curriculum than from a conscious effort to target global competency as a learning outcome for all students.

By the late 1990s the college had made some initial strides to broaden multiculturalism to include global diversity. As learning outcomes became more formalized in higher education, the college identified eight "core abilities" that should be integrated into the curriculum and college experience. Within that framework, global and domestic diversity were integrated as part of a core ability of "Global and Cultural Perspectives" (1996). Students were said to be developing global and cultural perspectives when they:

> Exhibit knowledge of basic global literacy including: geography, history, and similarities and differences among cultures; express sensitivity towards and respect for the complex range of experiences of diverse peoples including ethnicity, gender, social class, religion, nationality and age, and recognize the interdependence of societies with world economies, political systems and the environment. (Global and Cultural Perspectives, 1996)

This work drew on publications from the American Council for International Intercultural Education and the Stanley Foundation, which articulated a need for global competency in the community college environment (Educating for the Global Community, 1996).

Early studies, however, revealed that the core ability of Global and Cultural Perspectives (1996) was viewed by faculty as the least understood and least integrated into the fabric of education of the eight core abilities defined by the college. To address this shortfall, the college supported several small but important initiatives, including a guest lecture series of international speakers and the introduction of study-abroad programs through membership in a regional consortium.

Leveraging Regional Consortia.   Collaboration with other regional institutions was critical to leveraging these early efforts to establish a foundation for global learning at Madison College. Within the Wisconsin Technical College System (a decentralized network of 16 geographically defined districts), the Instructional Services Administrators committee (composed of chief academic officers of each district) established the State Standing Committee on International Education in 1994 and granted

NEW DIRECTIONS FOR COMMUNITY COLLEGES • DOI: 10.1002/cc

authority for that committee to spearhead international education efforts for the Wisconsin Technical College System (WTCS).

In 1996 the committee implemented a formal Developing a Curriculum (DACUM) process in which employers from key workforce sectors, including manufacturing, education, human services, and state and local government, were asked to identify critical global and multicultural duties and tasks needed in the contemporary workforce. The results, published under the title "World of International/Multicultural Work Skills," identified key "duties," including "global perspective, languages, communication, cultural integration, organizational effectiveness, and professional growth" (World of International/Multicultural Work Skills, 1996). For each of these duties, the DACUM identified a rubric of key skills, or "tasks," including "recognizing impact of global marketplace, recognizing the interdependence of the global community, developing a minimal understanding of a second language, managing culture stress (culture shock), and functioning as a cross-cultural team member."

Based on this employer-driven data, the WTCS Standing Committee for International Education led an effort to infuse the curriculum at Wisconsin technical colleges with greater depth and breadth of global content. The Standing Committee was awarded small but important grants from the WTCS board in 1997 and 1998. These awards provided minigrants for projects that would increase the capacity of the technical colleges to provide students with the global skills they would need to compete in the regional employment market and to provide regional businesses with the skilled workforce needed to adapt to the changing world economy. Through these grants, faculty from throughout the system produced 30 international curriculum development projects, and all 16 districts participated in some global or multicultural initiative. Madison College received funding as part of this award cycle to create a web page that served as a clearinghouse for information about all of the projects funded by the Standing Committee as well as a gateway to other early web resources for international and multicultural education.

Through another critical regional collaboration, Madison College was able to begin offering study-abroad programs to its students. In 1996 Madison College joined the Illinois Consortium for International Studies and Programs (ICISP), a regional organization open to colleges in Illinois and contiguous states. Founded in 1986, ICISP is one of the oldest regional consortia for study abroad, with membership of approximately 40 institutions offering semester and summer study-abroad programs, faculty exchange programs, and other initiatives. Originally founded by Illinois State University, by the 1990s ICISP had evolved into a predominantly community college consortium providing colleges that lacked the resources or ability to manage semester and summer study-abroad programs with a ready-made model for student exchange. Through ICISP, Madison College was able to offer students a portfolio of study-abroad opportunities that had been vetted by a regional consortium and curriculum that had already been articulated with Illinois Community College Board standards. This opportunity provided a critical bridge until Madison College eventually was able to create its own in-house study-abroad programs and exchange partnerships. Without leveraging the capacity of the regional consortium, Madison College would have lacked the staffing and infrastructure to adequately support the growth of study-abroad programs in the 1990s.

Staffing and Institutional Capacity.   Early Madison College efforts were completed largely by committee and an early 20% special assignment, but by 2002 the college had restructured a position to devote 50% time and effort to implementation of global education initiatives. This grew to a full-time position in 2005. The establishment of a position dedicated to internationalization proved to be a critical leverage point that allowed the college to evolve toward a robust model of comprehensive internationalization.

Today Madison College manages an integrated Center for International Education with six full-time and part-time staff (4.7 full-time equivalent). Internationalization efforts include study-abroad programs, international student admissions and services, globalization of the curriculum, and other related international education programs. Staffing has grown as the center has increased its capacity to generate revenue through international student admission, study-abroad program fees, and aggressive pursuit of grants and other external funds. None of this growth would have been possible, however, had the college not invested in a coordinator position early in the development of internationalization at the college. By establishing a dedicated individual to shepherd internationalization initiatives, advocate for internationalization strategy, and provide due diligence for health and safety for study-abroad programs, Madison College has been able to chart a steady pathway for growth of international activities.

Assessment and Continuous Improvement.   Critical to any internationalization effort is not only the process of establishing goals for global learning, but also a willingness of the institution to engage in assessment processes that spur continuous improvement. Madison College's internationalization strategy builds upon the American Council for Education (ACE) model of comprehensive internationalization in which assessment and data are regularly used to measure the process of internationalization (Olson, Green, & Hill, 2006). Assessment has included not only quantitative data on internationalization measures, but also a process of facilitated discussions with faculty, college leadership, and key stakeholders. That discussion process revealed hidden talent and expertise among faculty with strong backgrounds or interest in international activities that led to new partnerships and the growth of early faculty-led study-abroad programs. The dialogues also established a context within which to grow both grassroots and top-down support and understanding of internationalization initiatives.

In addition to regular self-study and benchmarking, in 2005 the college hired an external consultant to assess strategic internationalization and provide benchmarks for a new 5-year plan for internationalization. Recommendations of that report led to the integration of international student admissions within the Center for International Education where it could be given more dedicated attention and build synergy with other internationalization initiatives, a business plan for long-term solvency of the Center, and numerous policy and procedure modifications.

External Funding. A key strategy in the development of a business plan for the Center included pursuit of external funding to seed new initiatives and provide the short-term funding to create new programs for collegewide internationalization. Early efforts were rewarded with a number of small international project awards, including funding from the National Peace Foundation, the International Fund for Agricultural Development, the University of Wisconsin–Madison Center for International Business Education and Research, and Community Colleges for International Development.

An infusion of $180,000 in federal Title VI-A funding from the U.S. Department of Education via the Undergraduate International Studies and Foreign Language (UISFL) program ushered Madison College into a new level of comprehensive internationalization in 2007. Through the UISFL initiative, Madison College embarked on a comprehensive internationalization effort that included greater focus on world languages, professional and curriculum development support for faculty internationalization, and the establishment of an Interdisciplinary Global Studies Certificate.

Key to this process was an effort to engage faculty in updating course content to include international foci, drawing on ACE recommendations for internationalization at the disciplinary level (Green & Shoenberg, 2006). Via a partnership with the University of Wisconsin–Madison, two-semester sequences of both Arabic and Chinese language study were developed at Madison College and the college hosted nationally attended workshops related to both geographic areas of the world. Faculty in a broad range of disciplines were encouraged to develop new globally oriented courses or infuse global content into existing courses that could be linked with the newly established Interdisciplinary Global Studies Certificate. In all, 37 new courses were created and more than 80 courses were integrated to count toward the Interdisciplinary Global Studies Certificate.

Along with the expansion of internationalization initiatives, increased attention to internationalization of the curriculum also led to a greater sophistication in the development of global learning targets or competencies. Building on the earlier work of Madison College core abilities outcomes and the WTCS International Work Skills DACUM, the Madison College faculty and grant team drafted new learning outcomes to guide the implementation of the Interdisciplinary Global Studies Certificate. Divided into six categories of cultural awareness, intercultural communications, world languages, international travel, global citizenship, and global work skills, these competencies provided both students and faculty with clear definitions of global understanding (Global Learning Outcomes, 2008).

Faculty-Led Field Studies and Service Learning Programs. In a conscious effort to expand internationalization beyond humanities or general education disciplines, Madison College actively encouraged the growth of faculty-led study-abroad programs in vocational programs and science, technology, engineering, and mathematics (STEM) fields. A faculty training program in study-abroad leadership was developed and start-up funds were set aside as part of the Title VI UISFL award to create new field studies and service learning programs in less commonly internationalized fields.

Among the new courses created was a field studies course, Renewable Energy for the Developing World. This course leverages a similar college expansion in renewable energy curriculum development through a National Science Foundation award that established Madison College as a national trainer in renewable energy technologies via a network titled the Consortium for Education in Renewable Energy Technologies (CERET). Key faculty in the CERET initiative partnered with the Title VI grant team to create a course where students travel with faculty to a rural mountain region of Costa Rica to install solar panels on homes of individuals whose remote location or lack of economic means does not allow them to connect to the electrical grid. The credit-bearing course affiliated with this program allows students in engineering to gain a unique exposure to developing world social and cultural issues, and credits earned for the course count toward both the CERET and Global Studies certificates. The Costa Rica program was implemented in partnership with Solar Energy International, a nonprofit organization dedicated to education and training in renewable energy and sustainable building technologies, and the Rancho Mastatal Foundation, a Costa Rican eco-village that both provides a home base for student lodging and serves as a liaison with the local community.

Capacity Building for Study-Abroad Training Program. In September 2010, Madison College was selected by the U.S. Department of State's ECA for a Capacity Building for Study Abroad award that uses the Costa Rica Renewable Energy for the Developing World program as a model to train other community colleges in best practices in internationalization and study-abroad program development. The program is based on a scalable model in which eight faculty from community and technical colleges across the United States are competitively selected for subawards in which a faculty member from each institution travels to Costa Rica, participates in the Madison College service learning course, and experiences the program in action. This immersion in experiential education is followed by a yearlong program of online networking; a 3-day best practices in study-abroad development workshop; and connection to publications and resources for sample policies, procedures, and assessments of study-abroad and campus internationalization. In turn, each subawardee is expected to

NEW DIRECTIONS FOR COMMUNITY COLLEGES • DOI: 10.1002/cc

work with other colleges in the grant network to create a new short-term faculty-led service learning program related to renewable energy, engineering, or sustainable development. The target area for new program development is Central America and the Caribbean, with the expectation that lessons learned in Costa Rica will be widely applicable in that broad region and that travel costs for community college student participants will be minimized by keeping programs within a zone of relatively low-cost international airfare.

The State Department's stated goals of the Capacity Building for Study Abroad initiative are to "expand the institutional capacity of U.S. colleges to offer study abroad" and to "expand student opportunity for study abroad by increasing the number of non-traditional students, introducing non-traditional fields of study, and broadening offerings to non-traditional countries." By focusing on STEM fields at community colleges that have had limited or no study-abroad programs, the Madison College program squarely addresses these goals and leverages individual college efforts by creating a consortium that promotes intercollege collaboration. The Madison program also answers federal calls from the 100,000 Strong initiative and Lincoln Commission Report by expanding the capacity of community colleges to provide study-abroad opportunities in strategically targeted world regions and by increasing access for underrepresented students and STEM disciplines.

The network of institutions participating in this project has been dubbed the Community College Sustainable Development Network (CCSDN), and by 2013 has grown to include 24 community colleges across the United States from Hawaii to Maine. The network has launched new sustainable development programs in the Bahamas, Belize, Costa Rica, Honduras, Jamaica, and Nicaragua, as well as a sustainable foods program in Italy, and numerous other programs are currently in program development stages, including possible programs in India and South Africa.

Walking the Talk of Experiential Learning Models

A key factor in the design of the Madison College program is that the faculty selected to develop new programs do not travel to Costa Rica merely to observe the program or conduct a site visit. Rather, participants in the training are expected to work side by side with students during the service learning program. Faculty from academic backgrounds in agriculture, civil engineering, or even culinary arts join Madison students in learning to wire solar panels, fabricate roofing supports, and install LED lighting in rural locations.

This model of engagement is a critical and intentional aspect of training design. The goal is to immerse faculty in an experiential learning environment that actively models best practices in study-abroad program design. As such, we hope that faculty will be engaged and enthused about

international learning, that the barrier between student and faculty participants in the program will be blurred, and, most important, that the lessons
of study-abroad program development will be understood both in theory
and at the level of experiential practice. In short, we wanted to "walk
the talk" of experiential learning, not only with students, but also
with faculty who are engaged in global learning through professional
development.

Lessons From Experiential Learning Theory. Modern conceptual-
izations of experiential education owe much of their framework to the
work of John Dewey (1859–1952). James Citron and Rachael Kline sum-
marize the thrust of Dewey's contribution by his assertion that "the goal of
education is not to come up with the right answer—since that could
change—but rather to understand and use one's experiences" (Citron &
Kline, 2001). Dewey further articulated a learning model by which such
understanding and experience are linked to student learning through a
cycle of experience, reflection, testing of hypotheses through new experience, and finally a deep internalization of understanding that is based not
on rote theory, but upon practice and experience. Dewey's model has been
widely adapted and refined by numerous experiential learning scholars (see
Kolb, 1984), but at their core, almost all models of experiential learning
build on this cycle of action, reflection, and practice.

In addition to Dewey, the other figure whose work is most often cited
as a foundation for experiential learning is Kurt Hahn (1886–1974). Hahn
founded Outward Bound in 1941 as a nonprofit organization dedicated to
using experiential education to teach life skills of teamwork, confidence,
and responsibility. Key to Hahn's approach is the idea that the greatest lessons in experiential learning come when participants are challenged beyond
their comfort zones. Outward Bound courses, for example, often push
young urban participants to use newly learned wilderness survival skills as
a means to drive participants beyond their comfort zones and force them to
reassess their attitudes and behaviors. Many scholars have built upon
Hahn's model to argue that the most powerful experiential learning envi-
ronments are those in which students are pushed outside their normal rou-
tines and patterns of behavior, yet stop short of inducing paralyzing anxiety
(see Priest & Baille, 1995).

Study abroad likewise is founded on the principle that international
experiences force students to reassess their understandings of the world by
challenging comfortable cultural and behavioral norms. However, unless
we as international educators can integrate learning experiences that
encourage students to move outside their comfort zones and reflect on
activities that allow students the time and space to process and understand
these lessons, we cannot assume that international travel alone will prompt
students to question their worldviews or generate the lessons of global
understanding that we aspire to in the field. In fact, without attention to
experiential learning principles, we may run the risk of reproducing the

stereotypes of so-called ugly Americanism abroad where study abroad functions as little more than glorified tourism. Citron and Kline (2001) caution that without intentionality of experiential learning design, programs may suffer from a "consumerism effect" where students function as customers in a marketplace and colleges compete to offer fun and ultimately nonchallenging programs that increase numbers of students participating in programs abroad. Others have gone further to assert that uncritical study abroad may reproduce the elitism and distance of the colonial experience (Ogden, 2007–2008).

Experiential Learning in Costa Rica. During their training at Rancho Mastatal, faculty participants in the CCSDN program are often pushed outside their comfort zones. Rancho Mastatal is an immersive living lab for sustainable living. The ranch specializes in providing living examples of organic gardening and regional farming, local economic development, holistic health, natural building techniques, renewable energy systems, and other sustainable living activities. Accommodations during the program are very rustic. Faculty and students share bunk-style sleeping arrangements in open-air bamboo and wattle buildings. Cold showers, long hot days of work, and difficult hikes to carry in supplies and gear to remote installation sites are the norm. Toilets are open to the jungle and are either composting latrines or attached to a biogas digester, which provides methane used to fuel the kitchen stove. While most participants are awed at the example provided by Rancho Mastatal for living in harmony with the environment, they are also often unsettled by contrasts to their energy-wasteful lifestyles back home and forced to reflect on consumption decisions that are taken for granted by most American households.

For many faculty participants, this is also their first time traveling abroad with students. Even for those who have led groups abroad, most have not participated alongside students in experiential learning activities. This presents a rare opportunity for the dynamic of instructor and student to be inverted so that faculty are not in control of the learning experience. Furthermore, because faculty are selected from very diverse academic disciplines, the content of the service experience—wiring small-scale DC solar lighting systems—lies outside the academic sphere of expertise for most participants. Engineers accustomed to working on computerized blueprints and conservation ecologists used to identifying plants and animals work alongside students to string wires, fabricate makeshift light fixtures, and frequently look to students from renewable energy programs to share their expertise in making decisions during the projects.

In keeping with experiential learning design, reflection and discussion are key aspects of the training design. During the program, each day concludes with a group meal where participants are asked to share insights from the day. This nightly reflection and discussion culminates on the final day with a debriefing session in which students and faculty share insights and lessons learned from the program. Upon return, students in the program participate in an online course that includes reflection essays as well as other more technical or data-driven assignments, and faculty in the training program are networked via an online discussion forum and prompted by a formal postexperience survey to reflect on the learning of the program. Finally, 3 months after the completion of the Costa Rica travel, faculty participants in the CCSDN training are reunited in Madison for a 3-day workshop on best practices in study-abroad program development and design, in which faculty share insights and applications of their learning.

Assessment Results.   Madison College is currently in its third year of a 3-year CCSDN capacity building program. Sixteen separate colleges have completed the study-abroad training program in Costa Rica, and another eight faculty from new institutions are in Costa Rica at the time that this chapter is being written. With a sample size of only 16 institutions, it is impossible to gather statistically significant data from assessment responses. However, the assessment data gathered provide strong case study support for the model of experiential training described here.

All participants were asked to complete an online survey assessment both after the completion of their Costa Rica travel and after their best practices workshop in Madison. When asked if the program provided a model of excellence in study-abroad programming, all but one participant agreed or strongly agreed (one neutral response). All respondents (100%) indicated gain or significant gain in knowledge or understanding of program learning targets, including logistics related to study-abroad program development, safety and risk management abroad, group dynamics for study-abroad trips, study-abroad teaching strategies, and renewable energy abroad. Participants were also asked to self-assess their understanding of study-abroad program development on a scale from 1 (little or no understanding) to 5 (significant understanding) both before and after participation in the program. Before participation, the average faculty self-assessment ranking was 2.2. After participation in the program, the average faculty self-assessment of understanding had risen to 4.1, showing strong growth in faculty understanding. Finally, 100% of participants indicated that this training provided more hands-on experience than other activities they had attended in the prior 2 years, and 100% indicated that they were "very likely" (highest rating) to recommend the CCSDN training program to colleagues.

More telling than the numerical data are the faculty's open-ended responses. Overall feedback from program participants has been overwhelmingly positive, including such glowing reviews as:

"This was the most useful workshop I've ever attended! Never before have I gone to a training and ALL aspects of the discussion have applied to what I needed to know!"

"What an amazing program. I could really see this being the best way to encourage community colleges to increase or begin study-abroad programs."

"This really was one of the best workshops I've attended. The mix of formal and informal interaction was great. I really appreciate that time was made to promote interaction among the participants."

Moreover, most respondents specifically cited the experiential nature of the program as a key factor in their professional development. Being placed in the role of a student allowed them to internalize lessons of being outside their own comfort zones and reflect on program design from new perspectives:

"The time at Mastatal reminded me that being in a new place is an educational experience; the importance of study abroad is in this time of 'living outside your normal comfort zone' and meeting new people."

"Seeing how the students reacted to the material, living situation, etc. from a position that was essentially on par with them [was the most significant learning experience or insight]. It broke down many of the faculty-student barriers and allowed for very frank interactions with the students."

"This was one of those experiences where immersing yourself into a program makes you think about things and questions you never would have had you not been in the thick of it. This is an essential part of the training."

"I think that being put in with students and participating as a student was an invaluable way to understand the other side of a study-abroad program."

Conclusions

Today community colleges, like all higher education institutions, are compelled to provide students with the knowledge, skills, and attitudes they will need to be successful in life and work in a globally integrated community. The experience of Madison Area Technical College has been a gradual but strategic effort that has drawn upon best practices in comprehensive internationalization, experiential learning principles, and employer-driven data to define key strategies for holistic internationalization. Key elements of Madison College's success in internationalization have included the following seven best practices:

1. Strategic planning for internationalization includes clear goals and regular assessment.
2. A holistic model of internationalization allows the synergy of internationalization efforts to contribute to a whole that is greater than the sum of individual parts.
3. Faculty engagement at the level of academic discipline is key to integrating global learning into programs of study, especially for STEM or vocational studies.

4. Faculty-led study-abroad and service learning programs engage faculty and create discipline and career-relevant international learning experiences.
5. Experiential learning models help both students and faculty move beyond their comfort zones toward truly transformational learning experiences.
6. Successful internationalization is accompanied by a business plan that has allowed for growth of staff in proportion to the scope of internationalization efforts.
7. Use of regional consortia and external grant funding have leveraged each success toward larger and more comprehensive initiatives.

While this list is by no means meant to be inclusive of all best practices in community college internationalization, it is reflective of the path that Madison Area Technical College has taken to grow from nascent experiments in internationalization to serving as a national leader in comprehensive internationalization and faculty-led program development. This case represents a replicable and scalable model in which colleges with limited funding and human resources can establish internationalization goals that allow for strategic growth.

References

Citron, J., & Kline, R. (2001). From experience to experiential education: Taking study abroad outside the comfort zone. *International Educator* (Fall), 18–26.

Educating for the global community: A framework for community colleges. (1996). Arlie Center, Warrenton, VA: American Council for International Intercultural Education (ACIIE) and The Stanley Foundation.

Global and cultural perspectives. 1996 Madison Area Technical College. Retrieved from http://madisoncollege.edu/global-and-cultural-perspectives

Global competence and national needs: One million Americans studying abroad. (2005). Washington, DC: Commission on the Abraham Lincoln Study Abroad Fellowship Program.

Global learning outcomes. 2008 Madison Area Technical College. Retrieved from http://madisoncollege.edu/international/learning-outcomes

Green, M. F., & Shoenberg, R. (2006). *Where faculty live: Internationalizing the disciplines*. Washington, DC: American Council on Education.

Hayward, F. M., & Siaya, L. M. (2001). *A report on two national surveys about international education*. Washington, DC: American Council on Education.

Hayward, F. M., & Siaya, L. M. (2003). *Mapping internationalization on U.S. campuses*. Washington, DC: American Council on Education.

Kolb, D. (1984). *Experiential education*. Englewood Cliffs, NJ: Prentice Hall.

Mulholland, J. (2011, January 19). First Lady Michelle Obama says study abroad and "100,000 Strong" initiative make America stronger. Retrieved from http://blog.nafsa.org/2011/01/19/first-lady-michelle-obama-says-study-abroad-and-100000-strong-initiative-make-america-stronger/

Ogden, A. (2007–2008). The view from the veranda: Understanding today's colonial student. *Frontiers: The Interdisciplinary Journal of Study Abroad, 15* (Fall/Winter), 35–55.

Olson, C. L., Green, M. F., & Hill, B. A. (2006). *A handbook for advancing comprehensive internationalization: What institutions can do and what students should learn.* Washington, DC: American Council on Education.

Priest, S., & Baille, R. (1995). Justifying the risk to others: The real razor's edge. In K. Warren, M. Sakofs, & J. S. Hunt (Eds.), *The theory of experiential education* (pp. 307–316). Boulder, CO: Association for Experiential Education.

World of international/multicultural work skills. (1996, March). Wisconsin Technical College System, Standing Committee on International Education.

GEOFFREY W. BRADSHAW, PhD, is the director of International Education at Madison Area Technical College and the Project Director for the Community College Sustainable Development Network.

NEW DIRECTIONS FOR COMMUNITY COLLEGES • DOI: 10.1002/cc

5

This chapter is a story about one community college and how it transformed itself through comprehensive internationalization within the context of globalization.

Transforming International Education Through Institutional Capacity Building

Jack Bermingham, Margaret Ryan

In the 1990s, the forces of globalization began affecting community colleges and, in response, the internationalization of community colleges movement was set into motion. Though the mission of community colleges originally encompassed the local community, the distinction between local and global became blurred. Indeed, the "bifurcation of the global and local on both the discursive and lived levels is undergoing a transformation as it becomes less clear where one ends and the other begins" (Quint-Rapoport, 2006, p. 1). However, "global engagement has grown haphazardly and ad hoc" (American Council on Education [ACE], 2012) and efforts are falling short (ACE, 2012; Armstrong, 2005). Today, in spite of uneven results, community colleges have become important institutions in the development of global education. But what will it take for community colleges to reap the full benefits of internationalization?

A widely used definition of internationalization is that of Knight (2004): "The process of integrating an international, intercultural, and global dimension into the purpose, function, and delivery of post-secondary education" (p. 2). Knight qualifies the terms used in this definition. "With the notion of process, internationalization is conveyed as an ongoing effort; international recognizes nations, cultures, and countries, whereas intercultural reflects internationalization at home; and, global portrays a worldwide scope. Integrating connotes the institutionalization of internationalization. And, finally, purpose, functions, and delivery refer to the mission of postsecondary education" (pp. 11–12).

NEW DIRECTIONS FOR COMMUNITY COLLEGES, no. 161, Spring 2013 © 2013 Wiley Periodicals, Inc.
Published online in Wiley Online Library (wileyonlinelibrary.com) • DOI: 10.1002/cc.20048

To realize deeper and more thorough results, ACE (2012) advocates a new definition—a shift to what is referred to as comprehensive internationalization: "A strategic, coordinated process that seeks to align and integrate international policies, programs, and initiatives, and positions colleges and universities as more globally oriented and internationally connected" (p. 3). The ACE report claims that the synergy of an institutional commitment, administrative structure, curriculum and learning outcomes, faculty policies and practices, student mobility, and collaboration and partnerships would change the way practitioners think about internationalization—and therefore would influence institutional efforts. Comprehensive internationalization is therefore framed as a transformative process.

The definition of globalization used here is that of Levin (2001): "Globalization is both a condition (the world as a single place) and a process (linking localities to each other)" (p. 8). From the perspective that globalization is a "condition," downward forces pressure community colleges to respond with particular behaviors. Neoliberal ideology, the market economy, technology, and the increase in immigration are the predominant drivers of globalization forces. In Levin's theory of globalization, internationalization is categorized as a response to the condition of this central phenomenon. On the other hand, globalization as a "process" finds an "outlet within the community college with economic, cultural, and technological behaviors" (Levin, 2001, p. xiii). A debate ensues regarding whether organizational members are "passive recipients of globalizing changes or conscious, responsible actors, capable of forming intelligent and educationally beneficial responses to global conditions and processes" (Levin, 2001, p. 13). Different interpretations about the degree of agency that exists with regard to globalization are based on whether one adheres to the proposition that globalization is a condition or a process (Held & McGrew, 1999). Currently, the predominant perception is that the community college as an institution is capable of only reacting rather than demonstrating any agency (Cantwell, 2009).

This chapter is a story—from the perspective of a community college president—about one community college and how it transformed itself through the process of comprehensive internationalization within the context of globalization. With a commitment to preparing students to live and work in a global economy and multicultural world, the college designed its strategic plan to emphasize diverse and global perspectives in its curriculum and pedagogy—launching an innovative, organic process that has permeated the organizational structure and campus culture.

The story began in 1995 when Highline Community College developed a strategic plan that included the recognition that internationalization of the campus and curriculum as well as improving the college's response to diversity required a broad commitment. The plan informed activities that were targeted at industry clusters like global trade and information and communications technology and at rapidly changing demographics in local communities as priorities. College and faculty leaders realized that they needed to alter both the curriculum and their approach to teaching and learning to prepare students for job skills increasingly influenced by globalization.

Faculty Development

While faculty professional development is often self-directed, it can also be shaped by institutional priorities. Highline Community College expanded faculty professional development opportunities, in part, to give faculty international experience in addressing the new priorities. Highline's support for faculty development shifted to reflect changing global realities.

The college utilized its progress in building international partnerships and expanding its international student numbers. Resources gained from international student tuition were invested to support both international higher education partnerships and faculty development opportunities.

For example, the faculty exchange program with the prestigious Shanghai Jiao Tong University (SJTU) was created and relationships were expanded in Yangzhou, a sister city of a neighboring community. Participation in a trade mission to South Africa and Namibia provided formal ties to several institutions across higher education and training sectors.

College leaders also participated in several international conferences and joined professional associations that focused on international initiatives. The college hired a grant writer and contracted with academic experts outside the institution to facilitate workshops on curriculum initiatives and planning as the college strengthened internationalization inside and outside the classroom.

The college leadership and the board of trustees encouraged exploratory efforts in several countries. While not all of them led to a successful outcome, a few began lasting partnerships. As a community college in 1997, these early efforts provided a competitive advantage in seeking grant funding and legitimacy for internationalization as a priority.

College staff developed grant proposals that secured funds to support faculty development, curriculum initiatives, international partnerships, and international development projects. As international student numbers increased, more funding was earmarked for internationalization and its ties to educational excellence.

Broadening faculty capacity was critical to the success of these activities. Faculty expertise and innovation made sustaining responsiveness to changes in student and community engagement possible. Increasingly, the college's communities experienced an influx of immigrants and refugees, bringing a wealth of cultures and languages to the region. Classrooms filled with nonnative English speakers, who were representative of diverse

NEW DIRECTIONS FOR COMMUNITY COLLEGES • DOI: 10.1002/cc

cultures from Africa, Asia, Europe, and Latin America, and required different teaching strategies and broader content expertise from the faculty. Effective student engagement strategies necessitated new approaches to student success. This changing environment, the college's strategic plan, globalization, and the demands for a multicultural workforce all shaped a new vision for the institution.

Professional development that was dynamic, raised personal expectations, demanded new insights, and inspired deep commitment was essential to the college's success. Several faculty members and senior administrators were keen to participate in internationalization of the institution.

Progress relied on consensus on a few fundamental issues. In the early 1990s, faculty had agreed that a key student learning outcome needed to be a global perspective. A curriculum committee in the mid-1990s reinforced this expectation by recommending a course requirement with sufficient content to ensure this student outcome. These two steps compelled the institution to build the capacity necessary in the curriculum and with the faculty.

Experiential Professional Development: Early Days

Once Highline Community College's leadership emphasized the need for a global perspective as a core institutional initiative, *internationalization* in its most inclusive context emerged as the term reflecting the college's efforts. Since then, this word was often used interchangeably with *globalize* at the college. References to this terminology and its processes were evident in strategic plans, in the college's values, in student learning outcomes, in the core curriculum, and in the mission statement.

This institutional direction set Highline Community College apart from many higher education institutions, particularly community colleges. The college did not focus its international work in a single office. Many faculty and staff assumed implementation responsibilities. As with other higher education initiatives, faculty with expertise and those who are eager to become early adopters provided considerable momentum. Faculty division chairs and the faculty union leadership worked with administrators in academic affairs to increase capacity and build momentum for this priority.

For example, the college's exchange program with Shanghai Jiao Tong University (SJTU) gave Highline instructors from English, communication arts, journalism, and American studies the opportunity teach English language to top graduate students, most often doctoral students. At times, they also assisted SJTU colleagues in preparing manuscripts for publication in English. This successful partnership between an American community college and a prestigious Chinese university provided important credibility.

NEW DIRECTIONS FOR COMMUNITY COLLEGES • DOI: 10.1002/cc

During this same period, Highline deepened its presence in southern Africa. Building on previous personal and professional relationships, the college's leadership established memoranda of understanding with both the Polytechnic and the University in Namibia. The college partnered with a successful nongovernmental organization (NGO), Leaf College (later subsumed into the National Access Consortium Western Cape), in the Cape Town area that led to formal relationships with the province's universities and technical colleges. Emerging from former apartheid dominance, these institutions were interested in the American community college because of its access mission and its effectiveness in supporting economic development.

The technical colleges wanted to understand and utilize demand-driven curriculum, entrepreneurship, and business and industry relationships, as they planned to transform their roles in South Africa. The universities were focused on Highline's success in working with underprepared students who also came from ethnically diverse and economically challenged backgrounds. Each institution hoped to create capacity to offer contract training to pull funding from South Africa's new skills tax on industry.

Highline's formal relationships with these institutions positioned it to compete successfully for development funding through ACE's Higher Education for Development (HED; known earlier as ALO). The structure of these funded projects meant Highline faculty and academic administrators would work both in southern Africa and at Highline side by side with colleagues from these partner institutions.

These projects provided multifaceted opportunities for faculty development. While faculty on both sides of the partnerships were strongly committed to the success of the projects and were excited by the opportunity to travel and work abroad, they also focused on the far-reaching benefits from their experiences that expanded their perspectives on student engagement and changed their approaches in the classroom. Academic leaders structured opportunities for participants to reflect on the impacts of their project work as well as on their broader experiences. Those involved reported that professional development from these partnerships expanded capacity at each of the participating institutions.

When groups of colleagues from South Africa and Namibia came to Highline to work on projects, they were integrated into faculty professional development institutes in the college's Center for Learning and Teaching (CLT). This process was intended to deepen the reflective practice for all the institutes' participants. Faculty and staff teams worked together on project-related topics such as student retention, e-learning, entrepreneurship, curriculum development, and cultural competencies and learning styles.

The institutes' activities included several strategies to enhance faculty professional development. Some focused on characteristics of professional development evident in the participants' international experiences. The institutes enhanced camaraderie for all the international partner colleagues, deepening the impact on their perspectives and expertise.

In a sense, these educators discovered innovation in their new applied knowledge that broke new ground in developing added capacity for each partner institution. As participants in these development projects, they influenced the globalization of higher education.

Reflective practice and this new capacity materialized in many ways. For example, an instructor who taught human relations reported that she created a South Africa case study in her revised curriculum. The opportunity to craft a case study as a learning object was then supplemented with the faculty member's professional observations integrated into the case's analysis, and enriched by personal observations and experiences. It provided a new opportunity for the students to examine cultural contexts in terms of values and decision making that might relate to experiences with which they might better identify.

New awareness of the role of cultural competencies connected with the partners' interaction in development projects led the college's CLT to create a program to enhance these competencies for student and community engagement. Again, experiences gained in the development projects created strategies that improved student success on the campus.

Faculty became increasingly aware that their programs and disciplines were dominated by mainstream national and cultural perspectives. Several faculty members reported that their international experiences pushed them to broaden their disciplinary frameworks in their classroom teaching to incorporate the realities of globalization.

Pedagogical strategies like building community in the classroom and universal design for learning gained popularity in improving student engagement. Highline embraced them not only on its campus, but also as tools in assisting partner institutions to improve their student learning outcomes. For example, in one HED project in Namibia, faculty who worked closely with colleagues at the Polytechnic of Namibia on developing its Centre for Teaching and Learning (CTL) incorporated these strategies in its delivery priorities. International project experiences increased awareness of the institution's values and their significance for the students the college serves. Faculty members recognized that globalization was a dynamic process that dramatically influenced perspective and perception. Most important, they experienced the globalization of higher education as a force acting upon them and defining new relationships. Yet these faculty members and the college's leadership also shaped elements of globalization, as their project work took this community college abroad and influenced existing higher education institutions there. In some cases, these initiatives spurred other societies to create new institutions with similarities to the American community college. In a profound way, Highline faculty and administrative staff became part of globalization, and this work both strengthened and broadened the college's capacity.

Development as a Tool for Internationalization

The scope and impact of higher education partnership projects in southern Africa provided interesting opportunities to shape global education at the college and to create impacts that went well beyond the internationalization agenda envisioned in Highline's strategic plan. Institutions in a post-apartheid South Africa and Namibia demanded new models for higher education and training. The college's relationships in South Africa's Western Cape Province and in Namibia placed it in the middle of a rapidly changing environment that required thoughtful collaboration, respectful interaction, and partnerships characterized by equity.

By mid-1999, several Highline administrators and faculty members had worked successfully on the development of partnerships and on projects in both countries. At least 30 colleagues from institutions in southern Africa had visited Highline, many of whom worked closely with faculty during summer institutes or in collaborative workshops.

In 1999, the college received a Group Projects Abroad grant from the U.S. Department of Education that funded nine Highline faculty members to participate in a five-week "group Fulbright" to South Africa and Namibia. Because personal and professional relationships with Highline's partners were well established, faculty reported that they gained a much deeper understanding of education for development and its relevance to their responsibilities back at Highline. Partner institutions not only provided mentors and directed many content workshops, but also facilitated a number of community and student engagement opportunities. The program had all the best qualities of an immersion program.

Highline colleagues challenged themselves to pull as much from their experiences as possible and to reexamine their perspectives on the meaning of development and their roles as educators. Their program reports claimed that the depth of this experience transformed their perspectives and affected how they engaged students. For some, it also nurtured innovative approaches to the college's international partnership activities as they incorporated more from these experiences in defining new project opportunities.

Interestingly, this funded endeavor complemented the college's Department of Education Title VI-A and Title VI-B grants in advancing the type of professional development that transformed the college's curriculum and broadened student engagement. New courses were created and many existing courses received an infusion of internationalization. Faculty learning communities focused on international issues and the rubrics to assess the student learning outcomes they achieved. There were three strands that coalesced for the college, and by 2000, they were all evident. Faculty and academic administrators incorporated the lessons learned from the previous four years of international work to inform the next phase of internationalization.

NEW DIRECTIONS FOR COMMUNITY COLLEGES • DOI: 10.1002/cc

62 THE COMMUNITY COLLEGE IN A GLOBAL CONTEXT

The first strand was the path to addressing the student learning outcome of developing a global perspective as part of the degree requirements for the associate degree. Expectations for meeting criteria requiring significant course content and faculty expertise compelled the college to expand faculty development opportunities. The second strand was the support for faculty development in increasing the number of course offerings and in recasting existing curricula to respond to the requirement's criteria. The third strand evolved from the capacity-building work associated with the college's international partnerships. Faculty exchanges, project work, curriculum development, and mentoring abroad improved Highline's own capacity. These activities played prominent roles in instructors' approaches to teaching and learning. These experiences reinforced the faculty's pedagogical trend toward student engagement and community building inside and outside the classroom.

An unusual infrastructure emerged from the synergy in Highline's success in internationalization. Although grant activities were driven in part by project direction led from the office of the vice president for academic affairs, the synergy's strength was in internationalization's infusion across the institution. As a core value within the college that reinforced one of the institution's strategic initiatives, it gained broad support and its manifestations reflected an array of faculty implementation initiatives.

By 2001, the college had numerous overlapping projects in southern Africa. The impact of these activities and relationships spread to Highline's business and industry partners and several local professional associations. South Africa's ambassador to the United States visited the college four times and participated in business and industry events facilitated by Highline. Companies like Boeing and Paccar used the opportunity for one-on-one meetings with the ambassador. The college received assistance in getting approval for sending computer equipment and books to South African partner institutions on Boeing airplane deliveries to South African Airways.

The Namibian prime minister and the country's ambassador to the United States also visited. When Air Namibia purchased a Boeing 747, the prime minister, together with the finance minister and the ambassador, visited the college to thank the institution for its support of Namibia's interaction with Boeing and the college's successful partnership with the Polytechnic of Namibia. They were especially pleased that the college facilitated a cargo of computers and books with the airplane's delivery.

These relationships offered further examples of the globalization of higher education and its role in advancing economic development and international trade. The college's value to its business community in providing an entrée to influential decision makers in southern Africa heightened Highline's opportunities.

The college's momentum in its involvement in development projects set it apart from other institutions and established an important competitive advantage that provided access to business and political leaders. It also

NEW DIRECTIONS FOR COMMUNITY COLLEGES • DOI: 10.1002/cc

meant that some faculty members were positioned to strengthen their advisory committees as well as program support from business. Not coincidentally, the college received a substantial donation of computer hardware for its new computer center from Boeing.

Later, the college's strong program in international business leveraged its success in a partnership with Nelson Mandela Metro University (NMMU) in South Africa to gain the state's Center of Excellence for Global Trade and Supply Chain Management. This connected the college to an important industry cluster. The college benefited from the mutuality of these international partnerships. The opportunity that administrative staff and faculty created with their efforts to assist partner institutions enhanced the capacity of each participating institution, including Highline. Each funded development project in southern Africa reflected the priorities of the partner institution and Highline expertise. While Highline was providing technical assistance in support of USAID's mission, the college benefited from problem solving, curriculum development, and staff commitment and sense of purpose, strengthening Highline's capacity.

Two projects at the Polytechnic of Namibia illustrate this benefit. First, the Polytechnic sought to create its Centre for Entrepreneurial Development as a means to deliver contract training to business and government agencies. To build this capacity within the country at a public higher education institution allowed the country to leverage the resources expended for the training while enhancing local training expertise. Both reinvested capacity for the Polytechnic.

Highline's team for this project also pulled in American partner institutions to match the Polytechnic's needs. The additional benefit of this collaboration brought Highline fresh and innovative ideas to respond to local industry. Highline staff who worked on the project gained significant experience in understanding different business models. Faculty who worked with Namibian colleagues on curriculum development and facilitated Developing a Curriculum processes with Namibian industries also broadened their expertise.

The most impactful project for Highline was collaboration in the development of the Polytechnic's CTL. This project brought several faculty and academic leaders from Namibia to work with Highline colleagues, having an impact on more than 35 faculty as well as several key staff members. About 24 Highline faculty and academic administrators worked in Namibia on this project. Its impact provided Highline participants with a deep understanding of approaches to student success and the roles of the infrastructure in supporting this.

For example, Highline's directors of the library, instructional computing, e-learning, and the tutoring center each had reciprocal visits with their counterparts from the Polytechnic side. The Polytechnic was in the process of designing and building its new library and remodeling a structure to house the CTL. The deliberations about supporting the learning environment and the recognition of Highline's opportunity to rethink its approach and to draw on best practices across many institutions informed this work in Namibia and compelled revised strategies within Highline.

In a very similar fashion, faculty who worked on the CTL structure and program reviewed professional development frameworks and objectives. They looked at institutional priorities as well as staffing and expertise requirements. Highline faculty reviewed all their current methods and goals in their own CLT. Particular emphasis was placed on curriculum development and student engagement. Highline's work with gatekeeper courses in math and English along with its strategies for assessment of student learning attracted significant interest from Namibian colleagues.

The opportunity to host exchange faculty from both South Africa and Namibia during this work complemented the short-term visits from each side for Highline and southern Africa faculty. The visiting faculty participated fully in the discussions and pilot programs of pedagogical strategies that were emerging at Highline. The review of rubrics that clarified assessment and the modifications made, for example, in writing across the transfer curriculum and in professional-technical programs was enriched by input both at Highline and in Namibia.

As Highline's community became increasingly diverse with many non-native English speaking students, the college's faculty members revised their approaches in the classroom and their strategies that improved retention as they focused on these same issues in their work in Namibia on programming for the new CTL. Faculty reports on their activities in Namibia and on the changes they brought back into their own classrooms from their collaborations underscored the mutuality in this international partnership and the professional development gained on both sides.

In this period from 2001 to 2005, Highline probably reached its peak of international activities in terms of the breadth of participation and the momentum of change created at Highline. The opportunity to leverage another Title VI-A grant to broaden the internationalization efforts at the college and to respond to increasing evidence in the region of the forces of globalization was complemented by a new Title VI-B international business grant and a second Group Projects Abroad award for work in South Africa and Namibia. This external funding brought additional resources to engage new faculty at Highline and to add to the college's momentum in connecting more of its global activities to its own communities and to business and industry.

These initiatives funded 15 additional faculty members in an exchange role or for project work abroad. The Title VI funding strengthened the college's Chinese and Japanese language programs while supporting the implementation of Arabic language study. It expanded the capacity of the international business program and facilitated broad infusion of global topics in the business curriculum. These grants provided the groundwork to create the capacity to expand the globalism and diversity requirement to all professional-technical degrees. According to their project reports, faculty participation in the development work provided the kind of professional development experiences to have the confidence to infuse relevant global topics in their courses with the appropriate contexts. These changes were broadly evident in departments and programs such as business, engineering, computer science, paralegal, education, allied health, human relations, design, nursing, and hotel and hospitality management.

In the next four-year period, funding and international priorities shifted, but the impact on Highline of these types of international experiences continued and the momentum in enriching the campus learning environment grew. The southern Africa projects now included a complex partnership on educational access for the disabled. Highline drew on its long-standing success in working with students with intellectual disabilities. Its program focused on getting students jobs. Highline worked closely with False Bay College to develop the curriculum, enhance access at the college, and engage the students effectively. They partnered with three major insurance companies to create internship and employment opportunities. An NGO, the Disabled Peoples of South Africa, recruited the students and the University of Cape Town provided specialized services for them.

Highline also worked with False Bay College and Cape Peninsula University of Technology (CPUT) on an initiative that would eventually include participation from every further education and training (FET) institution and university in the Western Cape. The priority of this emerging consortium focused on contract training and matching training needs with programmatic capacity and proximity. Highline faculty and staff provided initial support for the timely development of demand-driven curricula.

Highline faculty from a variety of fields participated in an e-learning project that focused on using technology to infuse entrepreneurship across the science and engineering program at CPUT. They also participated in projects in both Namibia and South Africa that improved retention in engineering and the sciences and attracted more female students to these programs. The opportunities to tackle challenges like pass rates in first-year math and physics drew in many of Highline's math and science faculty. Faculty discussions focused on curriculum changes and improved strategies for student engagement. Highline gained other funding to improve its own student performance outcomes in engineering and computer science. Its support of students in these programs spurred ideas about supplemental instruction and mentoring strategies that filtered into the southern Africa projects. Highline's international partnerships and its faculty's success made the college more competitive in gaining external funding for projects at home.

NEW DIRECTIONS FOR COMMUNITY COLLEGES • DOI: 10.1002/cc

Consortium Initiatives

While Highline's leadership and innovative faculty initiated many of the projects and crafted several of the grant proposals, the international partnerships also gained much of their success through outstanding leadership at those institutions. Highline was able to collaborate with visionary leaders who expanded the partnerships and established strong "South-South" relations between Namibia and South Africa. For example, Tjama Tjivikua, rector of the Polytechnic of Namibia, clarified a practical reality in the globalization of higher education. He built his university through international engagement. He believed that for his institution to prepare students to be successful in the global economy and to contribute to Namibia's national development, he needed to establish partnerships around the world. These partners could provide access to funding, benchmarks to make certain his programs adequately prepared students, and strategies to lead Namibia into the knowledge economy.

Cassie Kruger, CEO of False Bay College, took advantage of the partnership with Highline in defining what a further education and training (FET) institution could become. His risk taking matched his commitment to outreach into disadvantaged communities. His openness to redefining access was an inspiration to many Highline colleagues and added to their motivation to make partnership activities relevant at home and successful in South Africa.

Martin Mulcahy, Joy Papier, Andre Mostert, and Seamus Needham each contributed to the development of the FET institutions. Perhaps more important, they crafted programs that provided access to postsecondary education for South Africans. Their partnership since 1996 with Highline guided the college's early development of its international relationships. They, together with Dr. Tjivikua, mentored Highline faculty and staff on ways to partner effectively and on strategies to engage in culturally appropriate relationships. As Highline expanded its international relationships, the lessons learned from these mentors facilitated an understanding of mutuality and a sense of authentic partnerships.

These leaders proved to be great partners in shaping higher education as part of globalization. Together with Highline, they charted a course of transformation as they sought to shape their destiny while defining their global engagement. They enriched Highline's efforts to internationalize while providing unique opportunities for professional development.

As Highline recognized the importance of these consortium relationships in southern Africa, the college's leadership also understood the necessity of participating in community college associations that would enhance its international capacity. The American Council for International Intercultural Education provided insight about relevant grant funding and potential mentor institutions in the United States.

Better opportunities emerged with a board membership in Community Colleges for International Development (CCID). Highline leveraged the resources and experiences of this organization to deepen and broaden its capacity. Highline faculty participated on several CCID international faculty development programs and senior administrator study tours that created new possibilities for partnerships and project work. Faculty participants reported acquisition of new skills for their classes and broader perspectives that enhanced their student engagement. These experiences also prepared faculty participants to work confidently with colleagues abroad on development projects.

CCID also opened doors to study-abroad participation. It collaborated on troika programs that pulled three member colleges together to share a program while rotating teaching staff. Highline faculty played a significant role in nursing in Ecuador and environmental science in Belize. CCID provided the faculty training for the programs and the infrastructure to make them successful.

CCID's offshore members also provided important networking chances, differing perspectives on partnerships, and experiences on development projects. The organization's capacity was instrumental in Highline's participation in several grants that have funded further internationalization of the college.

International Students

Highline has also taken on responsibilities for engaging international students in ways that support their development and complement their studies with service learning, leadership development, and lessons associated with American democracy and civic responsibility. These students have become a force for internationalization on the campus, in local schools, and in the community.

Highline's international student numbers have grown from less than 50 in the mid-1990s to over 300 by 2007. High-profile initiatives like the Community College Initiative (CCI) sponsored by the U.S. Department of State's Bureau of Educational and Cultural Affairs have catapulted these international students into the center of campus life. International students are involved in the formal student servant leadership program on campus. They have become outreach ambassadors and have spoken in the schools. They presented to state legislators, program advisory committees, and local service clubs; they lead student clubs and work closely with faculty.

The CCI students have organized the college's program for International Week and been active at many college events. Their visibility and engagement on the campus enhance the relationships with their mentor families and faculty advisers. They draw many faculty members to them and use those opportunities to discuss their experiences at home and their aspirations for the future. In most cases, faculty report that these students often have become leaders in the classroom, bringing their culture, perspectives, and experiences into the core educational environment. In a sense, CCI students, guided by project administrators and faculty mentors, increased the visibility of international students in contributing to the college's learning environment. They became an additional force of internationalization for the college and provided faculty with more tools to infuse global perspectives into their classes.

Highline also took the lead in proposing another dimension to the CCI program for Egypt and gained support from State Department and USAID funding. The Egypt Fellows Program brought faculty and administrators from Egypt's technical institutes to the United States for a 9-month experience at a community college. Highline provided 2 months of English language training, technology training, and an introduction to the American community college.

The Egyptian program's legacy provided the basis for a Highline international partnership in Egypt that led to a development project funded by the U.S. State Department. Also, it was the basis for Highline competing successfully for a similar project with faculty and administrators from Indonesian polytechnics. The ability of Highline's faculty to embrace these projects, learn from them, and deepen the institution's capacity continued to make the college's international work transformative for the institution and its learning environment.

New Capacity

As internationalization initiatives have transformed significant aspects of Highline, these efforts show some of the processes of the globalization of higher education unfolding. Yet it is also apparent that institutions like Highline demonstrate some agency in their work by shaping some strands of globalization and providing groundwork for potentially lasting institutional development in other countries. The possibilities of new community college–like institutions emerging out of Highline's global interactions provide exciting new opportunities for institutions like Highline that now have the capacity to assist countries in their planning and implementation.

For example, Highline has used its partnerships to offer industry-recognized credential programs through collaboration with partner universities abroad and has developed a dual degree-diploma program in China. It has also negotiated access to a formal doctorate degree program for administrators and faculty at Highline who may find this opportunity relevant for their career advancement and professional development.

The partnership with NMMU in Port Elizabeth, South Africa, provided the context for this innovative opportunity for Highline in development studies. One of Highline's doctoral-trained professors in economics teaches the prerequisites locally.

This international partnership with NMMU dates back to the university's support for Highline's "group Fulbright" programs. It was enhanced by a HED grant that targeted a new certificate program for NMMU in supply chain management. During this project, a group from Highline identified this possibility in the development studies program's structure. The program was financially affordable and was with a well-known university. Its delivery provided considerable flexibility for the student with no residency requirement. This example demonstrates one more way that the college's internationalization is a transformational force by creating new partnership initiatives.

Conclusion

Highline Community College in the Seattle metropolitan area has made internationalization an institutional priority since 1995. In examining the paths that the college followed in its activities designed to support and strengthen internationalization, it is evident that broad internal support, local workforce development needs, targeted financial resources, a talented and committed faculty and staff, large and diverse immigrant communities, and a region dependent on international trade for its prosperity were factors in the college's success.

Highline's aspirations reflected a commitment to an educational excellence that could not be defined without internationalization as both a core institutional value and a substantive student learning outcome. These beliefs were part of the college's values and mission.

The opportunities created by vibrant international partnerships, grant-funded projects and initiatives, and support from the college's leadership, along with the development work itself, resulted in changed attitudes, perspectives, and expectations.

Expertise emanating from reflective practice and these experiences guided an innovative internationalization. Perhaps Burch (2007) captures the broad participation in Highline's change:

> The individuals within the institution employ agency to reframe a problem. Strategies move from ad hoc and come to represent solutions unlike those offered by the status quo. The early signs of institutional change are guided by local, influential actors who have a vision in contrast to the status quo. These actors have the ability to identify common problems, develop alternative solutions, and build legitimacy for the solution by linking the innovation to established policy objectives and criteria. (p. 84)

While not fully comprehensive in its impact, internationalization emerged as a transformative force in the culture and climate of the institution. Its greatest impact was to change the learning environment so that it embraced global perspectives both inside and outside the classroom.

International engagement also had a significant impact on partner institutions, their communities, and their pedagogical approaches. In this context Highline Community College and its partner institutions shaped part of the globalization of higher education.

This story has demonstrated that internationalization is indeed a response to globalization. A comprehensive approach—particularly in the three areas of an articulated institutional commitment, curriculum and learning outcomes, and collaborations and partnerships—played a significant role in supporting and enhancing this institution's international capacity. Unlike ACE's recommended infrastructure and policies that seem more hierarchal, Highline's approach aligns with a campus culture that is more decentralized. Overall, these comprehensive internationalization areas, working together synergistically, should create significant benefits for community colleges.

The story of this community college illustrates a college ahead of its time for its achievement and innovation in comprehensive internationalization. Characterizing globalization as a process and approaching comprehensive internationalization as a strategy made the college an active participant of globalization.

References

American Council on Education (ACE). (2012). *Mapping internationalization on U.S. campuses: 2012 edition.* Retrieved from http://www.acenet.edu/news-room/Pages/2012-Mapping-Internationalization-on-U-S–Campuses.aspx

Armstrong, J. M. (2005). *The impact of short-term overseas assignments on community college faculty and staff* (Unpublished doctoral dissertation). School of Education, University of Iowa.

Burch, P. (2007). Educational policy and practice from the perspective of institutional theory: Crafting a wider lens. *Educational Researcher, 36*(2), 84–95.

Cantwell, B. (2009). *International post docs: Educational migration and academic production in a global market* (Unpublished doctoral dissertation). School of Education, University of Arizona.

Held, D., & McGrew, A. (1999). *Globalization theory: Approaches and controversies.* Malden, MA: Polity Press.

Knight, J. (2004). Internationalization remodeled: Definition, approaches and rationales. *Journal of Studies in International Education, 8*(5).

Levin, J. (2001). *Globalizing the community college: Strategies for change in the twenty-first century.* New York, NY: Palgrave.

Quint-Rapoport, M. (2006). The NGO-ization of community colleges: One (more) manifestation of globalization. *College Quarterly, 9* (Winter, 1). Retrieved from http://www.eric.ed.gov/PDFS/EJ835398.pdf

JACK BERMINGHAM *is the president of Highline Community College in Des Moines, Washington.*

MARGARET RYAN *is a professor in the business department at Highline Community College.*

6

This chapter provides a framework and recommendations for development of strategic partnerships in a variety of cultural contexts. Additionally, this study elucidates barriers and possibilities in interagency collaborations. Without careful consideration regarding strategic partnerships' approaches, functions, and goals, the ability to successfully implement international development projects is compromised.

Strategic Partnerships in International Development

Tod Treat, Mary Beth Hartenstine

As nations struggle to achieve sustainable economic growth and employment opportunities for a burgeoning youth population, many have established that a key systemic gap is the lack of an adequately trained workforce and a general lack of access to higher education opportunities. To address these challenges, some nations have entered into partnerships with educational institutions abroad that have had demonstrated success in improving these gaps. In the United States, community colleges have been the critical players in terms of creating greater access to higher education as well as being the core of workforce training for the country.

The U.S. community college represents a model of substantial interest in other countries due to its ability to respond quickly to community needs, its ability to address access and pipeline barriers to higher education, and, perhaps most important, its close working relationship with industry in meeting workforce development needs. Increasingly, U.S. community colleges are engaging in international development projects intended to build capacity both in partner institutions abroad and in the U.S. college itself. Accordingly, U.S. community colleges are positioned as major conduits for the transfer of knowledge to and from other nations.

Community colleges engaged in international development frequently turn to partnerships to increase project effectiveness and sustain activity. Such partnerships are inherently complex due to the wide array of interests both inside and outside formal governance. For example, ministries of

New Directions for Community Colleges, no. 161, Spring 2013 © 2013 Wiley Periodicals, Inc.
Published online in Wiley Online Library (wileyonlinelibrary.com) • DOI: 10.1002/cc.20049

71

higher education in particular countries may have interests in utilizing program participants in faculty development programs to increase the quality of higher education in the country, but may not be ready to support the infrastructure changes needed to implement and sustain ideas that might be incorporated by these participants. Development agencies in a funding role, in turn, may have developed expertise over time in attracting participants to U.S. programs, but not with a primary interest toward community colleges or the U.S. community college model. Funding agencies may have an interest in creating conditions for in-country change that are not shared by all partners. Nongovernmental organizations (NGOs) and for-profit firms may have expertise to provide support but very different aims. Finally, program deliverers must mediate these sometimes-competing interests while ensuring that each participant has the best possible experience and feels individual enrichment while at the same time recognizing opportunities for societal change in the home country.

This chapter provides a framework and recommendations for development of strategic partnerships in cross-cultural contexts. Without careful consideration regarding partnerships' approaches, functions, and goals, the ability of U.S. community colleges to successfully implement international development projects is compromised.

Analytic Framework

Strategic partnerships are often analyzed using the perspective of resource dependency theory, focusing on what resources, either intellectual or material, various partners can provide to achieve an aim (Barney, 1991; Iles & Yolles, 2003; Pfeffer & Salancik, 1978). Dependency theory suggests that partnerships exist in a fluid space in which partners sacrifice some of their autonomy though interdependence in order to exchange resources toward a common aim. Sustained partnerships require that potential power imbalances are continuously mediated, as such imbalances may lead to partner dependency, partner substitutability, and ultimate dissolution. Interorganizational learning among partners enhances a mutual, rather than one-sided, dependence that is sustained because the *relationship* is difficult to imitate, difficult to substitute, and durable.

Dependency theory often addresses the impact of partnerships on organizational performance, not the effectiveness of a program, and therefore is not able to provide sufficient scope of analysis to address mission-driven activity, such as international development. A particular shortcoming of resource dependence theory is a lack of attention to policy outcomes such as the public good, which may be important considerations for an international development project. Brinkerhoff and Brinkerhoff (2011) have developed a purpose-based taxonomy for public-private partnerships that address the public good. Their work suggests that a balance must be struck between benefits of partners and the public good. Such a balance is also relevant in the context of community college partnerships with other institutions, agencies, and systems, in which the benefits for each individual partner's constituents must be balanced. The taxonomy suggests that a decision must first be made as to the purpose of the partnerships: policy, service, infrastructure, capacity, or economic development. The normative principles that drive each of these purposes vary, as do the performance metrics that support them. For capacity-building partnerships, such as the partnerships described in this chapter, principles of ownership, empowerment, autonomy, and agency provide a foundation for success as measured by the transfer of knowledge and skills, building of systems and organizational infrastructure, and development of intellectual capital.

Fully developed partnerships demonstrate shared goal setting, development of trust and relationships, cooperative processes, decision making that is built on collaboration and partner strengths, shared responsibility, and shared results. Such partnerships result in function-driven communication, as opposed to hierarchical systems, and increased performance due to integration of activities.

International strategic partnerships have an added element of concern related to Hofstede's cultural dimensions—power distance, individualism or collectivism, assertiveness, uncertainty avoidance, long-term orientation, and (more recently) indulgence versus restraint (Hofstede, 2001). Hofstede's model suggests that attention must be paid to these dimensions at the partnership level to ensure congruence and shared understanding. Cultural competency on the part of organizational agents can effectively bridge misunderstandings, but cultural dimensions can play an important role both within and between country partnerships.

Finally, social capital, networks, and knowledge sharing are important elements for consideration in strategic partnerships. Amey et al. (Amey, Eddy, & Campbell, 2010; Amey, Eddy, & Ozaki, 2007) have used social capital constructs to address community college strategic partnerships, espousing development of network density, centrality, and trust as cornerstones of social capital development. In healthy partnerships, social capital emerges in the form of "partnership capital" in which trust and communication lead to integration and alignment of values, beliefs, practices, and processes between the partners. Inkpen and Tsang (2005) categorize these as cognitive and relational dimensions, both of which are needed in effective and sustained strategic partnerships. By situating strategic partnerships in network theory, Inkpen and Tsang are able to raise important questions about bounding, centrality, and knowledge flow that become very important considerations when organizations like community colleges are partnering with agencies and government entities. For example, if power dynamics move the community college partner to the periphery of a network knowledge flow, the community college can suffer, leading to deterioration of its role.

Utilization of each of these lenses to address strategic partnerships provides a comprehensive approach to address particular challenges found in international professional development or capacity-building programs in higher education. In particular, these lenses provide a rationale for choice of partners dependent on cultural context, project purpose, and desired outcomes, as well as informing dimensions of efficacy for partnerships once developed.

Principles for Effective Strategic Partnerships: Reducing Knowledge Gaps in International Development Partnerships

Effective strategic partnerships demonstrate an ability to consistently and efficiently convey common understandings, new learning, changes in approach, and problem solving across the partnership network. Eliminating knowledge gaps is not easy, however, and requires built trust, common goals, effective communication and alignment, and cross-cultural sustainability.

Trust.   While suggestions that good partnerships require trust seem commonplace, the importance of trust development to successful partnerships should not be underappreciated. Robson, Katsikeas, and Bello (2008) build a model of trust around both beliefs and behaviors that lead to increased effectiveness, efficiency, and responsiveness. Affective beliefs are those that are felt about a partner and can be built on through shared interaction and experience. Behaviors include receptivity to change based on partner influence; patience and cooperation (forbearance); and distributive fairness, which refers to the extent to which partners share responsibility, risk, and workload. Trust development for effective partnerships has been empirically shown to affect both partnership sustainability and performance (Robson et al.). Trust does not just evolve in strategic partnerships; it is earned through intentional action.

The factors for success in such arrangements are dependent on both the nature of the relationships and the kinds of organizations involved. The literature on international strategic partnerships characterizes these arrangements variously as joint ventures, bilateral or multilateral programs, public-private partnerships, alliances, and cross-sector collaborations. Each has specific advantages and challenges. A common factor to all arrangements, however, is the importance of developing personal relationships among organizational representatives to foster trust, openness, and cohesion and to avoid personality-driven conflicts. This focus on social capital within the relationships and networks of the partners is a foundational element of effective and sustainable strategic partnerships.

Partnership Goals and Assessment.   Aside from ensuring that program goals are clear among all partners, strategic partnerships also establish basic program goals for the partnerships themselves. These partnerships seek to ensure that (a) all partners are deeply committed to the cause of the program, (b) all partners are competent in their roles, and (c) all partners abide by a common set of communication principles aimed to advance the work of the project. High-performing partnerships demonstrate more advanced partnership development by ensuring further that (d) program goals have been determined through a collaborative process; (e) bidirectional communication structures occur at the level of work to avoid miscommunication through vertical, hierarchical structures; (f) partnership metrics address partnership efficiency, effectiveness, and ethics; and (g) results are based on collective contributions from all members of the partnership (Brinkerhoff & Brinkerhoff, 2011).

Communication and Alignment. The sustainable success of partnerships in international development relies on effective partnership communication and strategic alignment. In bilateral activities directly between two entities, such as two colleges or a U.S. community college and a nongovernmental agency in another country, communication and alignment require attention to the resource dependency needs of each partner and defined activities to support those needs. Multilateral projects present challenges of scale, scope, and complexity that are only partially addressed through the lessons of bilateral projects. Role clarity, communication, and alignment remain important, but the knowledge gaps in these partnerships produce cumulative, and often nonlinear, negative impacts. Effective alignment activities fulfilled by particular partners can reduce gaps that can negatively affect overall effectiveness. Many examples of successful bilateral and multilateral projects exist between U.S. colleges and universities and their international partners. In particular, Sutton and Obst's (2011) edited volume on strategic partnerships provides several case studies, including one community college. Particular themes of the volume, beyond the nuts and bolts of entering into agreements and principles of good practice, include moving from transactional to transformational partnerships, sustaining partnerships, and a managing partnerships portfolio to advance institutional interests. These themes resonate with community college international development as well, but the specific contexts in which community colleges frequently work deserve greater attention, as we attempt to provide in the remainder of this chapter.

In complex strategic partnerships, each entity has a defined role in implementation of the program but the roles cannot occur in isolation. In isolation, gaps in communication, shared understanding, troubleshooting, or goal consensus can reduce program efficacy (Treat, 2010). An example of such a complex, multilateral project is an international professional development program aimed at helping Egyptian educators and administrators better understand the U.S. community college model, teaching practices, and relationships with industry. The Instructors and Administrators of Egypt (IAE) program required close collaboration between five distinct entities and several colleges in both the United States and Egypt. The program funder, the U.S. Department of State's Bureau of Educational and Cultural Affairs selected the agencies that would be responsible for implementation. The Ministry of Higher Education in Egypt provided college contacts to coincide with reform efforts established internally. The Fulbright commission in Egypt recruited and selected participants. Community Colleges for International Development (CCID) designed program delivery in the United States through its central office and five U.S. community college members alongside various agencies that fulfilled specific roles.

Efforts to bridge gaps in projects such as the IAE program enhance the likelihood that the goals for sustainable change in the institutions in the home country are met. Involvement of the program provider with in-country partners, such as a ministry of higher education or NGO in the initial strategy of institutional participation, can result in selection of teams and institutions solicited to enhance change agency upon return. Beyond institutional selection, involvement in the selection of students, educators, and administrators with language skills, a greater propensity toward engagement with students and communities while participating, and a better understanding about expectations improves outcomes. Finally, enhanced involvement of the funder in coordinating, but not controlling, resource distribution and creating meaningful follow-on activities upon return can support the personal reintegration of students, educators, and administrators into society and support change.

Cross-Cultural Sustainability. Sustainability of strategic partnerships occurring in the context of international capacity building is affected by cultural factors, such as cultural and governance differences as addressed by Hofstede (2001). Cross-cultural sustainability aims to seek cultural match in values, expectations, communications, and desired outcomes. Relationship in cross-cultural relationships is essential to all of the partnership goals established earlier. Relationships engender behaviors that reduce friction, delay, and conflict in decision making. In addition, the resulting decisions are more impactful, increasing their value (Robson et al., 2008). Relationships can be complicated by differences in the way cultures learn (inductive or deductive), the way that cultures interact (direct or indirect), and what the culture values (individualism or collectivism). A low degree of match between cultures does not mean that partnerships cannot work, but does suggest that additional effort and relationship building may be necessary. Additionally, mismatched cultures must continue to work on partnership building to maintain both a relationship and project viability. Barkema and Vermeulen (1997) have addressed the negative impact of cultural distance on sustainability of international partnerships, which can be mitigated through repeated projects to maintain contact and reduce distance.

Learning From Experience and Implementing Improvements

A key element defining strategic partnerships is learning from previous projects and developing long-term relationships with partners through these projects to allow for both capacity building and resource assessment. Strategic partnership development recognizes that projects succeed, and fail, for a variety of reasons. Lack of success may be a consequence of mis-aligned partnerships, but may also be due to contextual factors, financial factors, or externalities that the program scope is unable to influence.

The Community College Faculty and Administrators of Indonesia (CCFA) program was modeled on the IAE program mentioned earlier, and many of the partners remained consistent between the two programs. Three observations regarding the IAE and CCFA programs are of particular note. First, context matters. Two very similar programs with a largely consistent group of partners produced markedly different results after the partners returned to their countries and institutions; these disparities were based on differences in the perceptions of institutional and individual autonomy, enthusiasm for change, and strength of commitment of in-country partners to expand the work.

Second, capacity and coordination matter. The institutions that partici-pated in the IAE program all had significant international development experience, including working with faculty and administrators. Despite this, program delivery was very complex due to variance in participant dis-ciplinary interests, variability of college programming and governance, and differential approaches to program delivery based on institutional practice and approaches. Consistency across the program was difficult to achieve.

Finally, learning matters. The mark of successful program improve-ment in strategic partnerships is the degree to which the partners learn, identify gaps in performance or outcomes, introduce interventions to address the gaps, and increase overall capacity. The challenge for CCID and the participant colleges in the IAE program was finding a way to accom-plish all four of these aims in a time frame that could demonstrate program improvement. Strategic partnership improvement, like program improve-ment, requires several cycles as organizations and institutions make appro-priate modifications. Learning is evident between the IAE and CCFA programs, particularly for those partners who remained consistent and incorporated lessons learned from one program to the next.

Assessing Strategic Partnerships in International Development

Saul, Davenport, and Ouellette (2010) suggest that members entering into strategic partnerships:

> have begun to take a more critical look at the value proposition of alliances in the context of the developing world. This pressure to demonstrate results is compounded by the very complexity of measuring partnership value. Partners and donors both struggle to measure not only how well a partner-ship is executed, but also how the alliance contributes to each partner's desired impact (whether development or business oriented). Furthermore, partners want to understand the incremental value of working in partner-ship. (p. 4)

NEW DIRECTIONS FOR COMMUNITY COLLEGES • DOI: 10.1002/cc

Successful evaluation of strategic partnerships must take into account a holistic focus on the overall impact of the program in which partners are rewarded for "contribution, not attribution." In other words, looking merely at cause and effect (did the partnership work or succeed in a specific objective?) in a complex partnership is not always attainable and in some cases not as meaningful an observation.

In successful strategic partnerships, each partner contributes according to its capabilities to fulfill the resource needs of the partnership, and the ability of each partner to meet its specific responsibility is subsumed by common efforts for overall program efficacy. Establishing outcomes that are measurable and creating metrics that focus on contributions of partnership members avoids two potential errors: supplanting activity for results, and replacing partnership effectiveness for effectiveness of individual members on discrete aspects of the program. Metrics limited to compliance audits fail to address the importance of improvement over the program cycle. Likewise, failure to identify metrics that address partnership effectiveness specifically precludes assessment of such important factors as capacity building, interorganizational learning, and longer-term outcomes.

Various metrics provide support for the work of strategic partnerships, but certain metrics are particularly valuable: those that focus on results, those that demonstrate additive value due to various partners' contributions, and those that measure enhanced efficacy of the partnerships themselves. An example of a contribution metric might be the number of faculty members adopting universal design for learning (UDL) elements in their classrooms after participating in a professional development activity. The result is in the application, not exposure through training. Incremental value metrics assess how contributions from various members of the partnership create additional value in the results. Successful implementation of UDL is enhanced, for example, by selection of institutions with progressive leadership, by identification of participants willing to learn and take risks, by effective UDL training and mentoring, and by support and troubleshooting when faculty attempt to implement UDL upon return to their home institution. Enhanced value of the partnership can be found in enhanced effectiveness, efficiency, scale, sustainability, order of change, or rate of change over the life span of the partnership.

Reaching appropriate metrics is accomplished by applying some of the principles of effective partnerships already discussed in this chapter: open channel of communications; intentional and explicit discussion to reach common understandings of program intentions and desired outcomes; expression of what each member is bringing to the partnership that enhances the overall efficacy; and, in particular, addressing the critical capabilities and valuable resources members bring that are not easily substituted, imitated, or otherwise acquired.

NEW DIRECTIONS FOR COMMUNITY COLLEGES • DOI: 10.1002/cc

Community College Partnerships

Community colleges are unique institutions that may be ideally suited for certain types of development and capacity-building projects. Workforce development projects are clearly a natural fit, but community colleges can also be ideal partners for capacity-building projects in the areas of community engagement, English as a second language training, developing short-term training responsive to community and industry needs (such as entrepreneurship certificates), and faculty and administrator professional development projects, among others. The participants who took part in the two projects described in this article were afforded opportunities simply not available in a less flexible university environment. The access they had to top-level administrators and the amount of time spent with faculty mentors and in the classroom are not likely to occur at a large university hosting such a project. The community of support that surrounded the program participants in these cases was unique. However, community colleges may face certain challenges in development work due to their structure and relatively small size. One clear example is a smaller infrastructure and staff to manage extensive reporting requirements involved with grant-funded development work: Large scale institutional grants systems and offices are not present at many community colleges.

Recommendations for Successful Community College International Strategic Partnerships

Take the long view: Begin partnerships with small projects, but build for large impact. Several chapters in this volume speak to institutional efforts to grow partnerships that began through simple exchange of ideas, short visits, a study abroad, or a faculty visit. Through sustained contact, idea sharing, and reciprocity, these relationships grow more complex opportunities. Repeated small projects with a partner have been shown to increase both trust and sustainability of a partnership (Barnes, 2011; Beckman, Haunschild, & Phillips, 2004; Xia, 2011).

Approach partnership development as a strategic portfolio. Partnerships can arise in a somewhat haphazard fashion, but strategic partnerships do not. Strategic partnerships consider needs and opportunities, seeking partnerships that complement their interests. A robust portfolio would ensure opportunity for faculty, staff, and students; ensure clear expectations and procedures through memoranda of understanding; provide geographical, cultural, and disciplinary diversity; and include a sustainability plan for faculty expertise, funding, and partnership development.

Recognize the implications of the origin of the funds and type of project. One cannot address strategic partnerships in the context of development work without looking at the genesis of the project. Is it a contracted training or a true development partnership? Whose idea was the project? Who approached whom? Were partners responding to a request for application from a government or foundation, or did one or all partners submit an unsolicited project idea to a potential funder? And, if the project is government funded, does it arise from public diplomacy motivations or from economic and social development motivations? Underlying all of these questions is whether the project itself fits the actual development needs or capacity-building needs of the partners.

Understand the partners. Understanding the strengths and weaknesses and underlying mission of each partner will improve the chances of creating a successful partnership. Governmental entities, such as the U.S. Department of State, Department of Education, USAID, U.S. embassies, or ministries of education globally are constrained by shifting political agendas, bureaucracy, legislative funding cycles, and frequent turnover of staff. Therefore, organizations or institutions entering into partnerships or funding relationships with these entities must be prepared for shake-ups or unexpected decisions. Communication tends to be more difficult than with a Fulbright commission because of the large number of projects and variety of partners and because embassies must deal with security and political challenges.

Fulbright commissions and other nonprofit education foundations rely heavily on government funding and are expected to respond to new government initiatives. As critical partners for the cases mentioned in this chapter, it has been important to understand how they function and how their participation in U.S. State Department–funded projects comes about. Also, it is important to have the buy-in of the commissions and the staff assigned to work on the project, and likewise the staff must have the latitude and authority to make programmatic recommendations and participate in decision making. Communication and relationship building between the implementers on the U.S. side (such as CCID and community colleges) and the commissions should be encouraged. The bilateral agencies (e.g., CCID and Fulbright) need to have a direct relationship, trust, and a clear understanding. It is critical to try to develop personal connections even though this is not necessarily expected by the structure of the funding or funding agency.

Hierarchical organizational structures lead to communication bottlenecks, and government-funded projects are particularly susceptible to this. Involving all partners in planning and respecting each partner's role in decision making and shaping the project allow for greater buy-in.

Finally, institutional partners have both internal considerations and a host of potential issues related to their *own* agencies and structures. Establishing direct partnerships with foreign governments or ministries or local educational institutions can be one way to streamline communication and project implementation, but also has its own set of challenges. Knowing who has the authority to make decisions is key; partners must be willing to accept changes to the nature and scope of the project based on limitations of the partner's authority to make systematic changes. Expectations must be made very clear at the outset. It is important to have shared values between the partners.

Discover and acknowledge motivation for participation. Determine who is benefiting from the project. Is there mutual benefit for all partners? Is there buy-in from key people at all institutions or agencies involved in the project? Some projects have multiple motivations, and the motivation may be different for the funder, the implementer, and the beneficiary. Higher education institutions may have conflicting motivations for participating in capacity-building partnerships depending on whether the project is mission-driven or profit-driven for the institution. The type of project—contract training or technical assistance versus a government-funded development project—will result in a very different outcome and a different partnership structure.

Recognize that unexpected outcomes may occur. Sometimes even with the best motivation, change or the stated outcome is not possible due to outside factors. In this case, project participants may seek alternative goals or benefits, and partners implementing the project may realize alternate benefits. Sustained partnerships expect the unexpected but also learn from the experience, incorporating learning into the next shared project.

Broaden the portfolio: Avoid single-source partnerships. Working to sustain strategic partnerships, individual organizations must also manage their partnerships to avoid becoming overly dependent on a single relationship. Ways of managing overdependence on a single relationship include forming additional partnerships with different organizations or by repeated, but changing, initiatives with existing partners (Beckman et al., 2004). New partnerships can insert competition into a partnership portfolio so that the individual organization does not become overly reliant on a single partner, while repeated partnerships build trust and enhance learning, which leads to reduced opportunity seeking and enhanced sustainability. At the same time, an individual organization's bargaining power in a relationship depends on its ability to provide valuable resources while learning at a rate commensurate with its partners to maintain partnership balance (Xia, 2011).

Conclusion

Strategic partnerships provide a useful tool for advancing international development work in the community college. The challenges and complexities of international development are rarely able to be completely mitigated by a single organization, but can be overcome by careful selection, cultivation and maintenance, role clarity, and measurement of strategic partnerships. Important factors are trust, motivation, clear outcomes, and shared expectations; in addition, the amount and type of resources contributed (staffing, time, money) and the intentional willingness of partners to develop patterns of belief, behavior, and assessment that advance partnership development is also critical. The strategic partnership model proposed in this chapter combines resource dependency, partnership purpose, consideration of cultural dimensions, and use of network theory as resources for developing a robust portfolio of strategic partnerships.

References

Amey, M. J., Eddy, P. L. & Campbell, T. G. (2010). Crossing boundaries: Creating community college partnerships to promote educational transitions. *Community College Review, 37*(4), 333–347.

Amey, M. J., Eddy, P. L., & Ozaki, C. C. (2007). Demands for partnership and collaboration in higher education: A model. In M. J. Amey (Ed.), *Collaborations across educational sectors*. New Directions for Community Colleges, no. 139. San Francisco, CA: Jossey-Bass.

Barkema, H. G., & Vermeulen, F. (1997). What differences in the cultural backgrounds of partners are detrimental for international joint ventures? *Journal of International Business Studies, 28,* 845–864.

Barnes, T. (2011). Intentionality in international engagement: Identifying potential strategic international partnerships. In S. B. Sutton, & D. Obst (Eds.). *Developing strategic international partnerships: Models for initiating and sustaining innovative institutional linkages.* New York, NY: Institute of International Education.

Barney, J. B. (1991). Firm resources and sustained competitive advantage. *Journal of Management, 17,* 99–120.

Beckman, C. M., Haunschild, P. R., & Phillips, D. J. (2004). Friends or strangers? Firm-specific uncertainty, market uncertainty, and network partner selection. *Organization Science, 15,* 259–275.

Brinkerhoff, D., & Brinkerhoff, J. M. (2011). Public-private partnerships: Perspectives on purposes, publicness, and good governance. *Public Administration and Development, 31,* 2–14.

Hofstede, G. (2001). *Culture's consequences: Comparing values, behaviors, institutions and organizations across nations* (2nd ed.). Thousand Oaks, CA: Sage.

Iles, P. A., & Yolles, M. (2003). International joint ventures, HRM and viable knowledge migration. *International Journal of HRM, 13*(14), 624–641.

Inkpen, A. C., & Tsang, E. W. K. (2005). Social capital, networks, and knowledge transfer. *Academy of Management Review, 30*(1), 146–165.

Pfeffer, J., & Salancik, G. R. (1978). *The external control of organizations: A resource dependence perspective.* New York, NY: Harper & Row.

Robson, M. J., Katsikeas, C. S., & Bello, D. C. (2008). Drivers and performance outcomes of trust in international strategic alliances: The role of organizational complexity. *Organization Science, 19*(4), 647–665.

Saul, J., Davenport, C., & Ouellette, A. (2010). *(Re)valuing public-private alliances: An outcomes-based solution.* United States Agency for International Development: Private Sector Alliances Division & Mission Measurement, LLC. Retrieved from http://pdf. usaid.gov/pdf_docs/PNADS458.pdf

Sutton, S. B., & Obst, D. (Eds.). (2011). *Developing strategic international partnerships: Models for initiating and sustaining innovative institutional linkages.* New York, NY: Institute of International Education.

Treat, T. (2010). Evaluating learning outcomes in an international professional development program. *Community College Journal of Research and Practice, 34*(1), 111–135.

Xia, J. (2011). Mutual dependence, partner substitutability, and repeated partnership: The survival of cross-border alliances. *Strategic Management Journal, 32,* 229–253.

TOD TREAT *is vice president for* Student and Academic Services *at Richland Community College in Decatur, Illinois, and adjunct assistant professor in the Department of Education Policy, Organization, and Leadership at the University of Illinois at Urbana–Champaign.*

MARY BETH HARTENSTINE *is project manager for the U.S. Department of State–funded Community College Initiative at Community Colleges for International Development, Inc.*

NEW DIRECTIONS FOR COMMUNITY COLLEGES • DOI: 10.1002/cc

7

This chapter describes the status of community colleges in Vietnam in the current context of the Vietnamese higher education system. Historical background and suggestions for the future development of Vietnamese community colleges are also provided.

The History and Future of Community Colleges in Vietnam

Anh T. Le

Since 1986, with the creation of the Renovation (*Doi moi*) policy, Vietnam has demonstrated a strong commitment to the improvement of its higher education system. After 25 years of opening its doors to the global educational environment, Vietnam has achieved some notable accomplishments. The country's higher educational system has become more diversified, more accessible, and more open to international cooperation. However, the management structure and quality assurance aspects of higher education still need significant improvement. One of the new and exciting opportunities for Vietnamese higher education is the development of community colleges. Even though colleges have long been a big part of the Vietnamese higher education system, most of them are specialized technical or vocational colleges. The emergence of community colleges, which resemble the U.S. community college model, is a fairly new phenomenon in Vietnam.

This chapter analyzes the literature and the Vietnamese government's policies regarding the direction of higher education in general and community colleges in particular. Predictions and recommendations for the future of Vietnamese community colleges are also provided.

The Higher Education Situation in Vietnam

Background Information on the Vietnamese National Educational System. Doan (2005) offers an overview of the history of the Vietnamese national educational system and its evolution through different stages,

New Directions for Community Colleges, no. 161, Spring 2013 © 2013 Wiley Periodicals, Inc.
Published online in Wiley Online Library (wileyonlinelibrary.com) • DOI: 10.1002/cc.20050

which correspond to national historical phases. For one millennium (111 BC to 939 AD), Vietnam was under Chinese domination. As a result, Chinese culture has the earliest and most significant influence on the culture and the educational philosophy of Vietnam. The philosophies of Confucianism, Taoism, and Buddhism have had a strong impact in the shaping of Vietnamese traditional education. Confucian teachings on the importance of virtue, social order, and harmony have been the foundation of Vietnamese culture and education. From 929 AD to 1858, Vietnam went through a series of Vietnamese ruling dynasties, but Chinese influence remained predominant in the national educational system.

During the period of 1858–1954, the educational system in Vietnam was mostly influenced by French ideology. One very important landmark in this period was the creation of the Vietnamese national language (*Quoc Ngu*), present-day Vietnamese. From 1954 to1975, Vietnam was split into two opposing states, with the North following the Soviet and Eastern European educational model and the South implementing the French and, later, American models (Binh, 2003). From 1965, the South of Vietnam experimented with the American model of higher education with the establishment of three multidisciplinary universities, three specialized private universities operated by various religious groups, and a number of community colleges. However, in 1975, the two states were reunified under the North state government and all the American-affiliated higher education institutions in the South were abolished. From 1975 to 1986, the whole country followed the Soviet model of highly centralized management in all spheres, including education. As a result, Vietnam suffered an economic crisis. In an effort to ameliorate the crisis, in 1986 the Vietnamese government decided to lead the country in a different direction through a bold move called *Doi moi* (Renovation). The government implemented innovative policies aimed at transforming the Vietnamese economy from a completely centralized system to a market economy with open policies for international relations (Dang & Nguyen, 2009). One of the major areas of transformation under this new direction was education. Since the adoption of the Renovation policy, Vietnam has been making impressive progress in increasing both the size and the quality of its national education system (Binh, 2003).

Current State of Vietnam Higher Education

National Education System.   According to the Vietnamese Ministry of Education and Training (MOET) website (MOET, 2006a), the current structure of Vietnam's national education system consists of six levels:

1. Crèches and kindergartens: ages 3 months to 6 years old.
2. Primary education (5 years): ages 6 to 11.
3. Lower secondary education (4 years): ages 11 to 15.

NEW DIRECTIONS FOR COMMUNITY COLLEGES • DOI: 10.1002/cc

4. Upper secondary education (3 years): ages 15 to 18. Alternatively, students can attend secondary technical and vocational education (3 to 4 years) instead of traditional high schools.
5. Higher education: junior college (3 years) and universities (4 to 6 years).
6. Postgraduate education: master's (2 years), doctor of philosophy (4 years).

In terms of administrative and financial aspects, Vietnam currently has four different kinds of educational institutions: public, semipublic, people-founded, and private. Public institutions are funded and controlled entirely by the government. Semipublic institutions are created, managed, and funded by the state in partnership with other economic or social organizations or with individuals. People-founded institutions are those established and operated by social or economic organizations.

The MOET is the ultimate authority in the Vietnamese education system. However, the degree of central control is different at each educational level. The primary and secondary education curricula are completely dictated by the MOET. The MOET still controls most of the essential aspects at the higher education level, such as the total number of credits and the percentage of core courses, as well as required courses and specialized courses for each field (Doan, 2005).

Since the implementation of the Renovation reform in 1986, Vietnam has made significant progress in improving the national education system. The total number of students has been increasing rapidly, from 20 million in 1996 to 23 million in 2005 (World Bank, 2012). Also according to the 2012 World Bank report on Vietnam educational development, Vietnam has achieved positive progress in ensuring the universalization of primary and lower secondary education. In the 2004–2005 school year, the participation rate of primary school-age children was 98.0%, and the transition rate from primary level (graduates) to lower secondary level (Grade 6) was 98.5%. From 2000 to 2005, 5.3 million people were trained in vocational training institutions, and the average rate of enrollment growth was 14.7% per year in professional secondary education.

Higher Education System. According to the 2012 World Bank report on Vietnam's educational development, the 1986 reform orientation for higher education emphasized new goals and structural changes in the sector. Training was provided for various economic components and to meet the diverse learning needs of the society. Instead of reliance on the state budget, all possible financial sources were to be mobilized and used. Instead of implementing only the planned targets set by the state, other non-state targets were also set and fulfilled. Instead of rigid training programs, various flexible and diverse training programs were developed to meet the requirements of employment creation and finding a job in a new market economy with many job-related changes.

One significant structural change was the merging of the various agencies into one agency that had sole authority and is responsible for the entire educational system. The aforementioned Ministry of Education and Training was established in 1990 from the merger of the Ministry of Education and the Ministry of Higher, Technical, and Vocational Education. The MOET has since been the main authority responsible for the national education system, which includes all levels from preschool to postgraduate programs (Ngo, 2006). In 1998, the Ministry of Labor, War Invalids, and Social Affairs assumed responsibility for vocational and technical education. The MOET controls most of the essential components of higher education, including the allocation of state funding and the setting of the curriculum. All academic matters are regulated by the MOET. Despite the MOET's significant power over higher education, other agencies are also involved. For example, universities of medicine and pharmacy are controlled by the Ministry of Health.

Based on training levels, higher education in Vietnam includes college education, university education, master's education, and doctoral education. College education offers training programs that are 1.5 to 3 years of study in duration. Colleges can offer less than baccalaureate training programs, whereas universities offer bachelor's, master's, and doctoral programs. Research Institutes can offer doctoral programs and, in cooperation with universities, can offer master's programs as permitted by the prime minister (MOET, Higher Education Department, 2006a). According to the General Statistics Office website (2012), in the 2011–2012 academic year there were 215 colleges and 204 universities in Vietnam. The total enrollment in higher education was 2,204,313, with 756,292 students enrolled in colleges and 1,448,021 students enrolled in universities.

Obtaining access to higher education in Vietnam can be very difficult because the demand outpaces the capacity of colleges and universities. Only a small percentage of those who pass the national entrance exam will be considered for matriculation. The difficulty in accessing higher education contributes to the persistence of inequalities in Vietnamese society. For example, London (2004) pointed out that in 1998, 18- to 23-year-old students from the wealthiest quintile were 61 times more likely to be enrolled than those from the poorest quintile.

The higher education entrance examinations are very competitive and stressful. The score on the exam is basically the only thing that determines eligibility for admission to colleges and universities. To prepare for this entrance exam, students usually start preparation programs at an after-school college prep center when they are in their junior year in high school. Until 2002, universities and colleges organized their own entrance examinations. In 2002, the MOET started and implemented a policy called "Three Things in Common" with the intention of improving access for students. The policy for all higher education institutions includes common use of examination items, common organization of examinations, and common use of examination results. The intention was to set a common standard for higher education entrance. Also, the common use of the results means that candidates can use their results to apply to various higher education institutions, instead of to just one as in the past (Ngo, 2006).

One of the priorities of the higher education reforms in Vietnam was to increase access to higher education. To this end, a number of other policies have been implemented, including:

- Setting different admission scores for different groups of students depending on their resident location: big cities, suburbs and towns, rural, and mountainous areas.
- Giving admission priority to children of war veterans and of ethnic minorities.
- Creating a preferential policy: Ethnic minorities can be accepted into some higher education institutions without having to take the entrance exam.
- Upgrading existing higher education institutions to increase their capacity.
- Expanding the size of the higher education sector through the establishment of new institutions, especially nonpublic institutions.
- Expanding the types of programs offered, especially professional and vocational programs.
- Implementing need-based student loan programs for low-income students.

As a result of these reforms, access to higher education in Vietnam has experienced some progress. However, expanding access still remains a big challenge for Vietnamese higher education. Hayden and Lam (2006) have noted that only 10% of the college-aged group is enrolled in higher education due to various barriers such as inadequate capacity and socioeconomic disadvantages. Geographic concentration may be a barrier as well: Out of the 150 universities, 102 are located in just five big cities: Can Tho, Da Nang, Ha Noi, Hai Phong, and Ho Chi Minh (MOET, 2009).

Community College: A Solution for the Reform of Vietnam Higher Education

Since the adoption of the Renovation policy of 1986, Vietnam has shown great effort to diversify its educational system so as to develop a skilled workforce to accommodate the new, freer market. The MOET has set a goal for vocational training at the higher education level of attracting 5% of students completing upper secondary level by 2005 and 10% by 2010 (MOET, 2006b). In the policy document, "Education Development Strategy for 2001 to 2010," the goals of higher education in Vietnam have been focused on connecting higher education training and society and market needs, seeking to do the following:

to provide high quality human resources in line with the socio-economic structure of the industrialization and modernization of the nation; enhance the competitiveness in fair co-operation for Vietnam in its international economic integration; to facilitate the expansion of postsecondary education through diversification of educational programs on the basis of a path-way system that is suitable for the structure of development, careers and employment, local and regional human resource needs and the training capacities of education institutions; to increase the appropriateness of the training to the employment needs of the society. (MOET, Higher Education Department, 2006b)

Since the United States and Vietnam trade agreement of 2001, Vietnam has experienced an explosion of demand for higher education. The global knowledge-based economy has created a strong need for higher education among Vietnamese youth. The national education system, both public and private, is facing extreme difficulty in accommodating the great increase in demand. The Vietnamese government has implemented a number of new policies to increase access to higher education, one of which is to expand in-service or part-time higher education. Until recently, most part-time students were government employees taking courses to update their skills as their work environment changed. However, more and more people are choosing this mode of education because admission is easier than the traditional path. Upon completing the programs, students receive a certificate (Ngo, 2006).

In a report on the development of the higher education system, the MOET (2009) acknowledged the progress of Vietnam's higher education system toward the goal of increasing access to higher education. The educational system has been diversified greatly in terms of ownership, training methods, training goals, and student composition. More sources of financial support for higher education have been mobilized. Higher education institutions have been built and distributed reasonably all over the country: 62 out of 63 provinces and cities have at least one college or university. The number of universities and colleges in the mountainous and disadvantaged socioeconomic areas has been increased, helping to create more opportunities for higher education for students in rural, remote, mountainous, and ethnic minority living areas. The number of nonpublic higher education institutions has increased sharply: In 1997 there were 15 nonpublic universities, but by May 2009 the number had increased to 81 institutions (44 universities and 37 colleges). According to regulations of the Law on Education in 1998 and 2005, the methods of colleges and universities were diversified, including regular official training and continuing education or nonofficial training (in-service training, distance learning, and self-study with instructions). The total number of students receiving regular training is nearly 900,000 students (of whom about 220,000 are distance learning students), accounting for approximately 50% of the total students enrolled in universities and colleges.

Despite the many progressive developments in Vietnam's higher education system, many limitations still exist. In comparison with other countries, the higher education attendance rate of Vietnam is still low. In 2006, the college-going rate in Vietnam for every 10,000 people was 166.5, whereas, using the same metric, in nearby Thailand the score was 374 (MOET, 2009). Obtaining access to higher education in Vietnam is extremely difficult due to the low pass rates of the university entrance examination (UEE). Out of the nearly 1 million students who take the UEE, about 600,000 students fail (Epperson, 2010). Even after passing the UEE, students must have high enough scores to be admitted into higher education institutions. The existing higher education institutions do not have enough capacity to accommodate all of those who pass the UEE. Oliver (2002) has stated that "only about 10% of the applicants that pass the national entrance examination can be admitted" (p. 4).

To widen access to higher education and strengthen the connection between higher education training and local and employer needs, the Vietnamese government designed a new model for higher education training, an alternative to the traditional university approach. The U.S. community college model was considered as a solution. The main characteristics of U.S. community colleges include:

• Designed to meet local needs.
• Open access, meaning a person does not need to earn a particular score on a standardized examination to enter the college.
• Institutional flexibility.
• Serving the under- or unserved.
• Noncompulsory.
• Lower tuition than universities.
• Awarding of certificates or degrees.
• Partnerships with local business and industry to meet their training needs (Epperson, 2010).

It was believed that community colleges could provide access to higher education for more people in Vietnam, especially those who live in rural areas. Also, community colleges can offer lower admission standards to give students who did not score high on the national university entrance exam a second chance at pursuing higher education. Just like the community colleges in the United States, most of the students attending Vietnamese community colleges are local youths seeking vocational training and short-term programs. In 1996, MOET submitted Report No. 8195/DH to the prime minister for directions to set up community colleges in Vietnam to offer local education to meet the demands of local workforce training. Community colleges were to offer programs ranging from short-term training courses to 2-year transfer programs. One main mission of the community colleges was to develop programs for professional training, vocational training, supplementary education, computer applications, and foreign languages (Dang & Nguyen, 2009).

Major Events in the Development of Community Colleges in Vietnam

The community college is still a fairly recent phenomenon in Vietnam; however, its roots can be traced back to the 1960s. From 1954 until the end of the Vietnam War in 1975, Vietnam was temporarily divided into two zones: the North followed the socialism model under the control of the Democratic Republic of Vietnam; the South was run by the Saigon government under the influence of the United States. In the 1960s, when peace talks were under way, the Republic of Vietnam in the South was eager to plan for reconstruction. The Saigon government invited U.S. consultants to help them in transforming the Vietnamese educational system from elite to mass education. The first community colleges were established in 1971: Tien Giang (Upper Delta) Community College in the Mekong Delta, and Duyen Hai (Coastal) Community College in the Central Region. The Saigon government utilized unneeded military and education facilities to house the community colleges. The community colleges were to offer six core programs similar to those of U.S. community colleges: occupational, transfer, remedial, guidance and counseling, general education, and adult education (Oliver, Engel, & Scorsone, 2008). Each community college had two faculties: the Faculty of Two-Year General Higher Education and the Faculty of Career Education. In the beginning, the Saigon government covered most of the expenditures, and tuition was free. Over time, other sources of financial support for the operation of community colleges were mobilized, including tuition fees, government funds (state and local), donations, businesses, and government agencies in and outside of Vietnam. During their short existence (from 1971 to 1975), the early community colleges mostly focused on career training to meet the labor needs of the communities.

After national reunification in 1975, the whole country was renamed the Socialist Republic of Vietnam and followed the Soviet model in most aspects, including higher education. Vietnam strictly followed the highly centralized, planned market model. Private education institutions were abolished. Interdisciplinary higher education institutions were transformed into mono-disciplinary universities to train state employees. The community colleges in the South were closed due to the lack of fit of the community college model with the Soviet ideology of education ideals. Community colleges also were thought to be too tightly tied with the United States (Dang & Nguyen, 2009).

Ten years into the Soviet model of the highly centralized, planned economy, Vietnam experienced a severe economic crisis. The Vietnamese government realized that drastic reform policies were needed to rescue the nation from crisis. Over two decades, a series of reforms have introduced principles of access, lifelong learning, and workforce development. In the early 1990s, a study tour of the Vietnamese Higher Education Delegation to North America was supported and sponsored by the U.S. Committee for Scientific Cooperation with Vietnam and by the American Association of Community Colleges. The study tour included visits to community colleges in Wisconsin and Illinois in the United States and the province of British Columbia in Canada. The delegation visited Thailand to tour some of its higher education institutions, as well. Lessons learned from the tour have been instrumental for the developing of the community college model in Vietnam (Dang & Nguyen, 2009).

In 2000, the temporary regulation of a community college by Resolution No. 37/2000/QD-BGD&DT of the Minister of MOET was established. The regulation states:

> Community college is a diversified public educational institution of the national education system: The local authority takes the responsibility for establishing, organizing, and operating training activities as well as scientific research on the basis of the regulation, aiming at meeting the demand of the local human force at the level of junior college or lower. (Dang & Nguyen, 2009, p. 101)

This resolution provided the legal foundation for the development of the first nine community colleges established from 2001 to 2005. In 2005, Resolution No. 25/2006/QD-BGD&DT modified the definition of community colleges as public educational institutions, for which local authorities take the responsibility of establishing, organizing, and operating training activities, as well as science-technology research aimed at meeting the demand for a skilled workforce in the community. They have a legally recognized position, like other colleges in the national education system. They offer diversified modes of training; provide links between learning levels inside and outside of the college in a wide variety of forms; connect training to application; and create a firm relationship between the college and local factories and enterprises, in particular where support of technology for farms, small and medium-scale processing mills of agricultural products, forestry and fisheries are concerned (Dang & Nguyen, 2009, p. 101).

Vietnamese community colleges are charged with the task of connecting families; the community; local authorities; unions; and cultural, economic, and social organizations in the local communities to promote training in professional skills, to connect theory and practice, to provide a bridge between training and vocation, and to improve the utilization of local resources for community development. Each community college's organizational structure is different and depends on the conditions and needs of the local community. These legal documents recognize the significant role of community colleges in the Vietnamese higher education system and give community colleges legal status and guidance for operation.

In 2009, the Vietnam Association of Community Colleges (VACC) was established. The VACC has joined the American Association of Community Colleges (AACC), and AACC is now a member of the VACC (VACC, 2012a, 2012b). The establishment of the VACC was a big achievement in the development of Vietnamese community colleges. The VACC is a strong indication of Vietnamese community colleges' consolidation and internationalization, as well as increased autonomy for the community college system. One important partnership of the VACC is with the Southeast Asian Ministers of Education Organization (SEAMEO). Established in 1965, SEAMEO comprises the ministers of education of Southeast Asian countries. The SEAMEO's main mission is to promote the development of the region through cooperation in education, science, and culture (VACC, 2010).

Current Status of Community Colleges in Vietnam

According to the VACC, the organization has 52 members, including universities, colleges, community colleges, educational centers, business units, and other institutions. All 13 community colleges are members of the VACC, which is the only authorized association for community colleges in Vietnam (VACC, 2012b).

Dang and Nguyen (2009) outlined the four major characteristics of the current Vietnamese community colleges. First, most of the community colleges are concentrated in the Mekong River Delta. Even though this area is thickly populated, the educational network is underdeveloped and most people of college age are not enrolled in higher education institutions. The students fortunate enough to be admitted to a university may have to move to the big cities. The financial burden of living in a big city, on top of tuition fees, is a strong barrier for many students.

The second characteristic is that the number of community colleges has been growing steadily. Between 2001 and 2012, 13 community colleges have been established.

The third characteristic is the gradually increasing enrollment at the community colleges. From 2002 to 2007, the total quota for college-level enrollment at the community colleges has increased fourfold.

The fourth characteristic is that the community colleges have a strong potential to meet the reform needs of Vietnamese higher education. The establishment of community colleges may alleviate some of the pressure surrounding acquisition of the necessary financial support from the central government. The community college model also gives local authorities more flexibility and autonomy in responding to local needs. In addition, the model emphasizes local and international collaboration to attract more financial and professional support. Community colleges could also potentially help reduce redundant consumption of resources by consolidating local higher and vocational institutions into one. MOET already has a plan in place to transform all local higher and vocational education institutions into community colleges (Dang & Nguyen, 2009).

Oliver, Pham, Elsner, Nguyen, and Do (2009) also provide a fairly comprehensive discussion of the characteristics of community colleges in Vietnam. The common characteristics they note are as follows.

Funding. Provincial funding is part of the community college's budget, but the largest contribution comes from other sources. Most of the college's funding comes from student tuition, training contracts with businesses, revenue from scientific research and services, and financial support from governmental and nongovernmental organizations.

Admissions. Due to the explosion of demand for higher education, the system is unable to accommodate every student who wishes to attend. Thus, the open admission feature of the U.S. community college model is not feasible for Vietnamese community colleges. To determine admission criteria, Vietnamese community colleges can either use the students' score on the national entrance examination controlled by MOET and administered by public universities or administer their own entrance examination. MOET also has issued a quota for each institution to determine the total number of students admitted. However, the community colleges usually admit a high percentage of the students who apply. For example, in 2006, Kien Giang Community College admitted nearly 86% of the students who took the entrance examination, and community college students made up approximately 70% of all of the province's postsecondary students. Similar to the U.S. model, Vietnamese community college students are generally from lower socioeconomic and minority groups. Nontraditional-aged students are also served through short-term programs for workforce development.

Programs. The community colleges are involved in the development of a wide variety of programs. Community colleges in Vietnam offer 3-year college programs, continuing education programs, vocational training, and certification programs. Although MOET has been cautious in approving transfer programs, they have been gaining popularity in recent years. So far, only a few universities are authorized to accept transfer students in limited fields of study. Among the participating universities are Can Tho University, Tra Vinh University, Hanoi Agricultural University, Nha Trang University, Nong Lam University, and the Ho Chi Minh City Technical Teacher Training University. The universities select the fields for transfer and request approval from MOET. The approved transfer fields of study include husbandry, instructional technology, finance, general accounting, aquaculture, business administration, electrical and civil engineering, and food processing and technology.

Globalization. Since their inception, the Vietnamese community colleges have been actively seeking international collaborations to help build the system and to exchange knowledge. Many of the VACC members and partners are international organizations. The VACC is intent on leading its members in the direction of globalization. Vietnamese community colleges are currently establishing many international partnerships in various forms. For example, the Saigon Institute of Technology (Saigon Tech) is affiliated with the Houston Community College District (Texas, U.S.A) and thus offers credits toward an associate's degree through Houston Community College. Another example is the partnership between Kien Giang Community College and the National Institute of Information Technology (NIIT) from India. Students at Kien Giang Community College can take courses offered by the NIIT and, upon completion of the 3-year program, can be awarded an international certificate by NIIT (Oliver, et al., 2009).

Challenges.   In general, Vietnamese community colleges have made much progress in introducing the concept of community colleges to Vietnam. The government (the MOET in particular) has come to realize the significant contribution and great potential of community colleges to the national reform of higher education. With the establishment of the VACC, community colleges have created an official coordinating body to represent them and to provide uniform guidelines and support. However, Vietnamese community colleges are also experiencing considerable confusion and uncertainty regarding their true place in higher education.

One sizable challenge for the development of Vietnamese community colleges is the lack of a clear legal framework to provide guidance and support for their operation and development. Because the community college model remains a fairly new phenomenon in Vietnam, the government, students, and the public are still skeptical of its effectiveness and quality. In addition, funding for community colleges is very limited (Dang & Nguyen, 2009).

Another challenge for community colleges in Vietnam is the mind-set that community colleges are inferior to universities. Parents and students usually do not consider a community college as their first choice. Some students who did not earn scores high enough to be admitted to a university will enroll in an extra year of a preparation program for the national entrance exam rather than apply to a community college. Even government officials subscribe to this mind-set. Many provincial leaders prefer having a university instead of a community college, in spite of feedback from local enterprises indicating that a community college would be an excellent fit for local human resource development needs (Oliver et al., 2008). As a result, some community colleges have been converted or upgraded to the status of a university.

There is also a dearth of qualified faculty for Vietnam's community colleges. Most community colleges are located in rural areas, making it much harder to attract qualified instructors. This is a problem for Vietnamese higher education in general, and one of its most daunting problems to solve

(Binh, 2003). According to Vietnam's 2012 educational statistics, at the university level, out of 59,672 teaching staff only 8,519 have a PhD; almost half (27,594) have a master's degree. At the college level, out of 24,437 instructors, more than half (14,696) have just a bachelor's degree, and only 633 instructors have a PhD (General Statistics Office, 2012).

Oliver (2002) argues that a centralized system with large bureaucracies, such as MOET, is hindering the development of community colleges in Vietnam. The large bureaucracies are distant from the local community being served by community colleges and thus are not able to respond promptly to rapidly changing local conditions. Also, the central government prefers uniformity across higher education to make administration easier, which hinders community colleges' ability to customize their programs to meet local conditions.

Transferring credits from community colleges to universities presents another challenge for community colleges. A lack of articulation agreements and the differences in entrance requirements between community colleges and universities are barriers for successful transferring of credits. The MOET also has not shown strong support for the transfer of credits from community colleges to universities for several reasons, including a lack of understanding of the community college model, concerns about the quality of community college graduates, and fear that the reputations of the universities would be damaged if the community colleges failed. Because most MOET officials were trained in the Soviet model, they have difficulty understanding the community college model. This lack of understanding continues to be a barrier for Vietnam's community college development (Oliver et al., 2008).

Future of Community Colleges in Vietnam

Community colleges in Vietnam are making steady progress in establishing their place in the higher education system. The government has recently shown more support for the development of community colleges. Most of the community colleges are active and vibrant, with strong presences through their websites and Facebook pages. Their programs and international collaborations are growing steadily. Given the great demand in Vietnam for higher education, it is likely that community colleges will become an essential part of Vietnamese higher education. Community colleges are regarded as a primary solution for increasing access to and quality of higher education (Dang & Nguyen, 2009).

Community colleges are gaining popularity in Vietnam. In the future, community colleges might become a priority for local authorities and the first choice for local students. However, the community colleges and the government in Vietnam still have a great deal of work to do to improve the conditions for community colleges. First, the government should give local committees permission to work with universities wanting to sponsor community colleges so that institutions can be more flexible in customizing their programs and curricula to meet the changing needs of the local community. Second, MOET should develop a clear legal framework to improve the management mechanisms needed to promote transferring programs, to attract more financial support, and to give community college administrators more autonomy in the operation of their institutions. Third, the community colleges need to improve the quality of their teaching staffs to ensure that they have the credentials and experience necessary to deliver qualified graduates. A high-quality teaching staff will also help to improve community colleges' reputations and image. Fourth, the VACC should develop complete accreditation standards and requirements, assessment and evaluation programs, and a better marketing campaign to raise awareness of community colleges. Also, the VACC should be the coordinating body to collect data about enrollment, graduation rates, and program development. These data will help the government understand community colleges better and could be utilized in the future to assess and develop new programs. Fifth, financial incentives, such as tax breaks, should be given to those businesses that work with community colleges to help train students and provide internships and jobs after graduation. Sixth, and finally, the government should encourage knowledge sharing between Vietnam and other developing countries who are also building their community college system, so that they may learn from and support one another.

References

Binh, T. (2003). Education reform and economic development in Vietnam. In T. Binh & C. D. Pham (Eds.), *Education reform and economic development in Vietnam* (pp. 214–231). London, England: RoutledgeCurzon.

Dang, B. L., & Nguyen, H. V. (2009). The development of the community college model in Vietnam at the time of the country's reorganization and international integration. In R. L. Raby & E. J. Valeau (Eds.), *Community college models: Globalization and higher education reform* (pp. 91–110). London, England: Springer.

Doan, H. D. (2005). Moral education or political education in the Vietnamese educational system? *Journal of Moral Education, 34*(4), 451–463.

Epperson, C. K. (2010). *An analysis of the community college concept in the socialist republic of Viet Nam* (Unpublished doctoral dissertation). University of Missouri–St. Louis.

General Statistics Office. (2012). *Giáo dục, Y tế, Văn hóa và đời sống: Giáo dục đại học và cao đẳng* (November data set). Retrieved from http://www.gso.gov.vn/default.aspx?tabid=395&idmid=3&ItemID=12674

Hayden, M., & Lam, Q. T. (2006). A 2020 vision for higher education in Vietnam. *International Higher Education, 44*, 11–13. Retrieved from http://www.bc.edu/content/dam/files/research_sites/cihe/pdf/IHEpdfs/ihe44.pdf

London, J. (2004). Rethinking Vietnam's mass education and health systems. In D. McCargo (Ed.), *Rethinking Vietnam* (pp. 127–142). London, England: RoutledgeCurzon.

MOET (Ministry of Education and Technology). (2006a). *Education landscape.* Retrieved from http://en.moet.gov.vn/?page=6.7&view=3401

MOET. (2006b). *The development goals of other levels.* Retrieved from http://en.moet.gov.vn/?page=6.1&type=&page=6.1&view=3458

MOET, Higher Education Department. (2006a). *Higher education in Vietnam.* Retrieved from http://en.moet.gov.vn/?page=6.7&view=4404

MOET, Higher Education Department. (2006b). *Higher education in Vietnam.* Retrieved from http://en.moet.gov.vn/?page=6.13&view=4404

MOET. (2009). *Report on the development of the higher education system, the solutions to ensure quality assurance and improve of education quality.* Retrieved from http://en.moet.gov.vn/?page=6.13&view=19831)

Ngo, D. D. (2006). Viet Nam. In *Higher education in South-East Asia* (pp. 219–250). Asia-Pacific Programme of Educational Innovation for Development, United Nations Educational, Scientific and Cultural Organization. Bangkok, Thailand: UNESCO Bangkok. Retrieved from http://unesdoc.unesco.org/images/0014/001465/146541e.pdf

Oliver, D. E. (2002). The US community college model and Vietnam's higher education system. Paper presented at the Fourth Triennial Vietnam Symposium, Texas Tech University, Lubbock, Texas, April 11–13, 2002. Retrieved from http://www.vietnam.ttu.edu/events/2002_Symposium/2002Papers_files/oliver.htm

Oliver, D. E., Engel, S., & Scorsone, A. (2008). Community college development in Vietnam: A global and local dialectic. In P. A. Elsner, G. R. Boggs, & J. T. Irwin (Eds.), *Global development of community colleges, technical colleges, and further education programs* (pp. 175–185). Washington, DC: Community College Press.

Oliver, D. E., Pham, X. T., Elsner, P. A., Nguyen, T. T. P., and Do, Q. T. (2009). Globalization of higher education and community colleges in Vietnam. In R. L. Raby and E. J. Valeau (Eds.), *Community college models: Globalization and higher education reform* (pp. 197–217). London, England: Springer.

VACC (Vietnam Association of Community Colleges). (2012a). Hiệp hội Cao đẳng Cộng đồng Việt Nam tổ chức Hội nghị về Quy chế Cao đẳng Cộng đồng. Retrieved from http://vacc.org.vn/index.php?page=news&do=detail&category_id=162&news_id=641

VACC. (2012b). *Introduction of Viet Nam Association of Community Colleges.* Retrieved from http://vacc.org.vn/index.php?page=news&do=detail&category_id=186&news_id=577

VACC. (2010). *SEAMEO RETRAC.* Retrieved from http://vacc.org.vn/index.php?page=news&do=detail&category_id=207&news_id=275

World Bank. (2012). Education in Vietnam: Development history, challenges and solutions. Retrieved from http://siteresources.worldbank.org/EDUCATION/Resources/278200-1121703274255/1439264-1153425508901/Education_Vietnam_Development.pdf

ANH T. LE is a PhD student in the Department of Educational Administration at the University of Nebraska-Lincoln.

8

This chapter focuses on the country of Tunisia and explores the possibility of bringing aspects of the American community college to the country to bring about needed reform and relief from unemployment.

Bringing Community Colleges to Tunisia

Linda Serra Hagedorn, Wafa Thabet Mezghani

Background

The country of Tunisia experienced intense uprisings and massive civil resistance that were termed the Arab Spring of 2010. The riots stemmed from a desire to topple government rulers who were blamed for the high unemployment, poverty, regional inequalities, and general political unrest within the country. In a quest for relief and prosperity, eyes are turning toward finding new alternatives that could solve the country's current problems. The American community college model is among the responses suggested to be tested, tried, and possibly followed. It is the community college's vocational aspects and its ties to business and industry that hold promise of contributing to relief of Tunisia's current difficult situation.

In this chapter we begin with a brief history of the country to better understand the current economic, political, and educational situation in Tunisia. We also provide background on geography, demographics, and the current political and economic situation, as well as a thorough description of the country's educational system. Finally, we describe a project to bring the community college to the country with the hopes and expectations that it can be a harbinger of friendship, peace, and stability. Tunisia is presented as a pilot example of using the community college model to bring economic development and hope that may be successfully replicated elsewhere.

History. Tunisia has a rich and long history. The earliest writings from the region of the current Tunisia record the arrival of the Phoenicians in the eighth century BC and the founding of the city-state of Carthage (Hunt,

New Directions for Community Colleges, no. 161, Spring 2013 © 2013 Wiley Periodicals, Inc.
Published online in Wiley Online Library (wileyonlinelibrary.com) • DOI: 10.1002/cc.20051

2009). Subsequently, the Roman, Byzantine, Arab, and Ottoman empires occupied the land. From 1881 to 1956, the area was a French protectorate. Modern-day Tunisia was declared a republic when it won its independence from France in 1956. However, the country has remained culturally and economically close to France. Tunisia's first president, Habib Bourguiba (in office 1957–1987), was responsible for expanding education and making it compulsory (U.S. Department of State, 2012). Tunisia's next president, Zine al-Abidine Ben Ali, rose to power through a 1987 coup. Although he is credited with bringing positive economic changes to Tunisia, he also brought back some of the earlier political repressions (Perkins, 2004; Profile, 2011). He was able to win reelection in 1994, 1999, 2004, and 2009 (Perkins, 2004) but was forced to flee to Saudi Arabia in 2011, accused and convicted of theft and possession of drugs, weapons, and priceless Tunisian antiquities (Adetunji, 2011). He was later also accused and convicted in absentia of murder and inciting violence, and his formerly imposed sentence of 35 years was extended to life in prison (Byrne, 2012).

At the time of this writing (early 2013), Tunisia is being ruled by an interim president, Moncef Marzouki. According to some, Marzouki presents a different form of president, being more soft-spoken and holding a looser grip of control of the country (Inkseep, 2012). This former doctor and human rights activist, however, inherited a country with high unemployment and relatively low wages for its workforce.

Geography and Demographics. Tunisia is nestled between Algeria to the west and Libya to the south and is only about 200 miles south of Italy across the Mediterranean Sea. The smallest of the North African countries, it has a land mass of approximately 63,170 square miles (National Institute of Statistics—Tunisia, 2012). In population, Tunisia is home to approximately the same number of inhabitants as the U.S. state of Ohio (some 11 million people). Its people are almost exclusively Arab, with Arabic the official language. However, due to the historical ties with France, the French language is very common. The most current birthrate per 1,000 persons is 17.28, ranking Tunisia in the middle as country 116 out of the 229 of those included in the Central Intelligence Agency's *World Factbook* (2012). The literacy rate is 74.3%, with the female rate lagging that of males by 18.1% (Central Intelligence Agency, 2012).

Throughout its history, Tunisia has been known as a moderate Islamic country. However, as a result of the earlier regime's political and religious oppression (though no official changes have been made so far in its constitution), the postrevolution era is witnessing an increasing interest in fundamentalism among certain groups.

Education. Tunisia has a compulsory education law for children ages 6 to 16. Designed after the French model, the Tunisian education structure is divided into kindergarten (ages 3 to 6 years); primary (Grades 1 to 6); lower secondary or preparatory (Grades 7 to 9), secondary (4 years), and postsecondary.

New Directions for Community Colleges • DOI: 10.1002/cc

To attend college, all students take a national exam called the bacca-laureate. Because admission to the public institutions is centrally controlled, all students who desire to attend college will be admitted to a postsecondary institution; however, only those with the highest scores will be granted admission to the top colleges or the colleges of their choice. Adding more uncertainty to access, there are quotas for the number of students who can be placed within each field of study (Education, Audiovisual and Culture Executive Agency [EACEA], 2012).

All but 44 of Tunisia's 195 universities are public and under state control (Ministry of Higher Education and Scientific Research [MHESR], 2012). Thirty of the public universities are under co-supervision of other ministries such as Health, Communication Technologies, social affairs, Agriculture and Hydraulic Resources, or others (MHESR, 2012). The remaining public institutions are under the supervision of MHESR. Since 2006, in conjunction with the Bologna Declaration, Tunisia adopted the French LMD system of degrees: bachelor (licence), master (maître), and doctorate (doctorat). Degrees or diplomas are also referred to as cycles:

First cycle: *Diploma d'etudes universitaires du premier cycle*—undergraduate level
Second cycle: *Maîtrise*—equivalent to a master's degree, graduate level
Third cycle: *Diploma d'etudes approfondies*—master of advanced studies or doctorate level

ISETs. Another Tunisian postsecondary option is the Higher Institutes of Technological Studies (*Instituts Supérieurs des Etudes Technologiques*, or ISETs). Classified under the General Directorate of Technological Studies, the 24 ISETs are under the supervision of the General Office of Technological Studies (also called the General Directorate of ISETs). The ISETs offer short-term professional programs that are generally more flexible and connected to the needs of the economy. Table 8.1 provides information on the departments and types of positions ISET graduates may hold.

ISET students participate in at least two internships during their 3 years of enrollment. The student generally serves as a laborer in the first internship and as a technician during the second. Upon program completion, ISET students earn a vocational bachelor's degree (*licence appliqué*), a terminal degree designed to lead directly to work.

Postsecondary Costs and Financial Aid. It is important to note that Tunisian public university education is free to all those who pass the national exam. Expenses related to books, supplies, lodging, and food are borne by the students and their families; however, the Tunisian government subsidizes both campus food and student health insurance. While the public university dormitories are less expensive than private housing, students

Table 8.1   ISET Departments and Positions

Department	Sectors	Examples of Employment of Graduates
Science of Economics and Management (SEM)	Commerce, industry, or general services	Accountant, management assistant, quality controller, human resources assistant, sales representative, import-export assistant, transit agent, shipping agent, or other related position
Computer Technology (CT)	Commerce, industry, or general services	Service and management of computer parks, program development, network design and wiring, network administration, diagnosis and supervision of industrial systems
Process Engineering (PE)	Chemical, pharmaceutical, oil, food security and hygiene, agro alimentary	Process driver, production supervisor or manager, research assistant, laboratory or development technician
Mechanical Engineering (ME)	Industrial maintenance, engineering or design, inspection, petrochemicals, mechanical construction, mechanical manufacturing, metalworking, transformation or processing quality control, management production	Production or maintenance technician, manager
Civil Engineering (CE)	Buildings, construction, road and urban infrastructure	Building technician, construction manager

generally can stay in the dormitories for only 1 or 2 years before having to move to more expensive options.

The Tunisian types and levels of financial aid are quite different from those available in the United States. There are a limited number of grants for low-income students that provide scant amounts of financial support (EACEA, 2012). The grants, typically around 50 TD (Tunisian dinars) per month, cannot stretch far when some textbooks cost as much as 60 TD. There are also limited loans available that are to be paid after the student graduates and finds employment.[1]

As a result of the Arab Spring, the transition/interim government initiated a new program called AMAL (*amal* is Arabic for hope) to assist unemployed university graduates. In addition to limited training to make the graduate more marketable, the program provides medical insurance and a modest payment of 200 TD per month (the equivalent of less than $130) for no more than 1 year. However, to be eligible for this program, the graduate must apply at the government employment office, be over the age of 28, have earned the degree at least 2 years ago, and have majored in one of a small list of specialties that carry a low probability of employment. This program was revised in March 2012 and given a new name, 3AMAL. Despite its noble goal of supporting those who are trained but unemployed, the program's future is uncertain due to its high government costs and difficulty in reaching a large number of university graduates (TN-Médias, 2012).

The Political and Economic Situation.   Before the Arab Spring and the Tunisian revolution (December 17, 2010, to January 14, 2011), the problem of youth employment attracted meager interest from policy makers and stakeholders. It was the suicide of college-educated Mohamed Bouazizi, a street vendor selling vegetables from a pushcart, that exposed the problem of unemployment and prompted people to scrutinize the true situation of the lack of jobs for the country's college-educated youth (Abouzeid, 2011). The naked truth came to the surface, revealing that the previously submitted and embellished figures masked the high rate of unemployment among the country's young, educated workforce.

The resulting social unrest, street demonstrations, and strikes were in protest of perceived social injustices, regional exclusion, poverty, and unemployment. Official elections held in late October 2011 for the National Constituent Assembly (NCA) resulted in the victory of Tunisia's Islamic Ennahda party (International Foundation for Electoral Systems, 2011). The NCA is charged with drafting a new constitution for Tunisia's new era. It is almost a certainty that the new coalition will face many challenges, the most important of which are the recovery of the economy and the employment of youth (World Bank, 2012).

Unemployment is a very serious and vexing problem. Escalating from 13% in 2010 (Index Mundi, 2012) to 19% in 2011 (World Bank, 2012), it is as high as 44% for recent college graduates (Wolf & Lefévre, 2012). Although there is evidence that the unemployment rate is declining slowly, the young and educated unemployed remain angered and dissatisfied.

The Tunisian situation raises a series of vexing questions regarding the roots and determinants of the high unemployment among the skilled labor force. Is the high level of unemployment due to a simple lack of jobs, cronyism and anticompetitive practices, occupational imbalances of worker training and employment opportunities, or an overemphasis on high-level and specialized education? Has the offering of free postsecondary education led to an inflated supply of specialized high-level workers that simply exceeds the demand? Does the responsibility for employment rest with the state, the university system, or the graduates and job seekers? These questions do not lend themselves to easy answers. Furthermore, to alleviate the situation will require change at the political, economic, educational, and social levels.

From the social perspective, people in Tunisia—especially parents— highly value those occupations related to medicine and engineering. Parents encourage their children to become doctors or engineers and to pursue graduate degrees even though there are insufficient jobs for the current lot of highly trained professionals in these fields (Haouas, Sayre, & Yagoubi, 2012). Despite a relatively large number of available jobs in agriculture and tourism, these fields are not culturally respected due in part to their seasonal nature. The aversion for jobs in these fields is such that most young people would rather choose unemployment over working in these areas. In addition, most Tunisians do not understand the practices required to find a job. They have not been taught the art of building a network, searching for a new job, or how to appropriately self-market to their advantage. And all of this occurs in a country without any kind of financial unemployment assistance.

From a policy perspective, hard answers may include policies tightly restricting the number of students allowed to enter the universities or actively directing students to specific programs of study more in line with the country's employment sector. Some policy makers turn for answers to changes in Tunisia's educational structure, looking at a unique type of educational institution to enable the education of a middle level of professionals such as technicians and skilled and semiskilled workers. Policies enacting this type of educational option would likely win the support of experts who attend job fairs and human resource expositions and who have identified a disconnect between education, acquired skills, and jobs available to young Tunisian workers.

From a political perspective, administration support in the form of financial aid or seed money may be required to enable young entrepreneurs to start new businesses and bring their ideas to life. The government must acknowledge its role in changing the status quo by enacting the policies that will not only redirect the unemployed toward training in different fields, but also provide the funding to make it an attractive option.

From an economic perspective, Tunisia must find a way to rebuild a balanced and competitive economy through education in strong and diverse areas, including mining, agriculture, petroleum products, manufacturing, and tourism. Research from the global management company Booz & Company, based on its work with Middle Eastern governments, confirms that "a sustainable economy enhances a nation's standard of living by creating wealth and jobs, encouraging the development of new knowledge and technology, and helping to ensure a stable political climate" (Shediac, Abouchakra, Moujaes, & Najjar, 2008, p. 1).

Can Community Colleges Contribute to Tunisia's Recovery?   It is naive to suggest that community colleges or any other single entity can single-handedly solve a problem as complex as the societal, political, and economic issues confronting Tunisia. Furthermore, the Tunisian government and its people would understandably scoff at progressive imperialistic approaches that would merely transplant the American community college onto Tunisian soil. However, Tunisia may find special benefits from studying the American successes (as well as the nonsuccesses) utilizing community colleges as the conduit for training and subsequent employment. Creating a Tunisian style of institution that bears resemblance to the American community college may be one tool used along with others to create an avenue of relief to the country's unemployment situation. A fully Tunisian postsecondary option must take into consideration the country's history, government structure, economics, social venue, and intended purpose. After all, the pressures leading to the consideration of community colleges in Tunisia are very different from those leading to their creation in the United States. Community colleges were expanded in the United States to increase access and postsecondary training to a wider group of Americans. It can be argued that the Tunisian problem is the obverse. In Tunisia the combination of free postsecondary education and ample access may have led to too many people attending college and graduate school, creating an overabundance of highly educated, but under- or unemployed graduates.

U.S. Embassy and U.S. University Linkage Program. In April 2012, the U.S. Embassy in Tunis, Tunisia, issued a request for applications related to U.S.–Tunisian university collaboration in five fields. One option, the "Comprehensive Community College Concept," requested a linkage between the ISET of Sfax[2] and an American community college to provide information and training on the American model. Kirkwood Community College in Cedar Rapids, Iowa, partnering with Iowa State University, and AMIDEAST[3] were selected to collaborate with ISET Sfax to provide a comprehensive program to guide Tunisians as they examine, experience, and consider the United States' unique community college educational model for their country's educational and economic benefit. The goal of the project was to provide experiential learning for Tunisians about the community college model and to develop a continuing relationship that will provide support for the future. The program provides two institutes for a team of Tunisian faculty and administrators. The Tunisians arrived in Iowa in February 2013 and visited the campuses of community colleges and businesses, learning firsthand about the establishment of community colleges and how to create partnerships with local industries. They were also instructed on the community college mission, as well as lessons related to institutional finance and governance. After leaving with projects to complete back home, the team will return to the United States in April 2014 to continue implementation plans for a new Tunisian postsecondary option.

This U.S.-supported collaboration begins a thought and action process and tests the robustness and flexibility of the community college model.

New Directions for Community Colleges • DOI: 10.1002/cc

The project also provides an opportunity to watch an idea move across the world and to test the parameters of its utility.

The Hard Work.   In some ways, it could be said that this road was traveled before in the United States. Tunisia's current situation can be likened to that of the United States going back about eight decades. During the country's era of the highest unemployment to date, the Great Depression, a number of emergency junior colleges were erected in various states to combat the dire economic situation (Diener, 1986). In most cases, the colleges were created using federal monies from the Federal Emergency Relief Administration and "proposed largely to serve unemployed high school graduates" as well as "putting to work those teachers and professors who were in the ranks of the unemployed" (Diener, 1986, p. 119). Typically, these emergency colleges were housed in high schools or in donated spaces after hours. The paths of these colleges varied by state, but overall they found a niche for Americans who utilized their services.

President Truman recognized the great value of the junior colleges, as recorded in the report *Higher Education for American Democracy* (President's Commission on Higher Education, 1947). In the six-volume report, frequently referred to as the Truman Report, the Commission recommended the name *community college* for institutions designed to serve the needs of the local community. Unlike the earlier junior colleges, the report recommended that community colleges offer terminal and semiprofessional education that included but would not be limited to vocational training. In the definition of semiprofessional training, the report emphasized that the colleges would also attend to the training of workers who had been in the workforce for any number of years.

The history of the origin of American community colleges identifies the conditions that may be instructive to Tunisia as the country considers community colleges. Fretwell's classic 1954 book on junior colleges included an appendix for communities to use when considering if the establishment of a junior college is appropriate. The index consists of seven major questions, each with several subquestions. We have revised and updated Fretwell's questions to provide a more contemporary and global perspective:

1. Is there a true recognition of a problem and the belief that education can be a part of the solution?
2. Are there individuals or groups who will take ownership and will champion the cause? Fretwell (1954) identified such individuals as "prime movers."
3. Will there be a federal response both in financial support and in acknowledgment of the importance of community colleges?
4. Is there readiness and support from local businesses?
5. Will the culture embrace the utility of lifelong learning and the need for retraining for workers of all ages?

NEW DIRECTIONS FOR COMMUNITY COLLEGES • DOI: 10.1002/cc

6. Can the new institutions have strong ties with the private workforce?
7. Can true synergetic partnerships be established with Tunisian business and industry?

We contend that these are important questions that the government and policy makers of Tunisia must confront. Of course, if it is determined that community colleges can offer great benefit to Tunisia, the next set of questions would address the specifics of a financial structure to support the colleges, policies on governance, decisions on where the colleges would be located, how they would be funded, and the creation of a compensation policy for the faculty. Perhaps the biggest policy issues would concern how the culture would create and establish a culture of acceptance.

Conclusions

Tunisia's complex situation will take substantial time, money, and ideas to improve. As indicated earlier and as suggested by a study by the Carnegie Middle East Center (Achy, 2011), Tunisia faces significant key problems, including "young unemployment, a large number of marginal jobs, increasing income inequality, and substantial regional disparities" (p. 1). Issues of this magnitude require more than just a new postsecondary option.

When the proposal to the U.S. Embassy project was originally written, the American authors believed that the establishment of community colleges could greatly alleviate the issues confronting Tunisia. But as the project progresses and as we learn more about the country and its historical, political, economic, financial, and cultural realities, we recognize that while the concepts related to the American community colleges may be instructive, a postsecondary response must be wholly Tunisian and be developed only after a careful needs assessment and market analyses are performed. Moreover, options such as revisions or additions to the current Tunisian ISETs may be a logical next step. Such revisions would carefully consider and nurture stronger ties with local industries and more purposefully foster workforce development in the vicinity. If change is to happen and if community college ideals are imported, change must come from Tunisian ingenuity and investment. While the American partners may be eager to assist, they must remain cognizant that the power and the authority to enact change, to establish new institutions, and to create a stronger link between education and the workforce lies with Tunisians. But, with the help of the U.S. Embassy support, we do look forward to seeing positive results.

Notes

1. The interest rate on loans is very low.
2. Sfax is Tunisia's second largest city, with a population of approximately 400,000.
3. AMIDEAST is an American nonprofit organization whose mission includes "Preparing individuals for jobs in the global economy" (AMIDEAST, 2012).

References

Abouzeid, R. (2011, January 21). Bouazizi: The man who set himself and Tunisia on fire. *Time*. Retrieved from http://www.time.com/time/magazine/article/0,9171,2044723,00. html

Achy, L. (2011). Tunisia's economic challenges. Retrieved from http://carnegieendowment. org/files/tunisia_economy.pdf

Adetunji, J. (2011, June 20). Ben Ali sentenced to 35 years in jail. *The Guardian*. Retrieved from http://www.guardian.co.uk/world/2011/jun/20/ben-ali-sentenced-35-years-jail

AMIDEAST. (2012). About AMIDEAST mission. Retrieved from http://amideast.org/about/how-amideast-making-difference

Byrne, E. (2012, June 13). Zine al-Abidine Ben Ali gets life sentence for role in Tunisian killings. *The Guardian*. Retrieved from http://www.guardian.co.uk/world/2012/jun/13/tunisian-court-punishment-zine-al-abidine-ben-ali

Central Intelligence Agency. (2012). *The world factbook*. Retrieved from https://www.cia. gov/library/publications/the-world-factbook/rankorder/2054rank.html?country Name=Tunisia&countryCode=ts&regionCode=afr&rank=116#ts

Diener, T. (1986). *Growth of an American invention*. Westport, CT: Greenwood Press.

Education, Audioivisual and Culture Executive Agency—Unit P10 Tempus (EACEA). (2012). *Higher education in Tunisia*. Retrieved from http://eacea.ec.europa.eu/tempus/participating_countries/overview/tunisia_tempus_country_fiche_final.pdf

Fretwell, E. K., Jr. (1954). *Founding public junior colleges: Local initiative in six communities*. New York, NY: Teachers College, Columbia University.

Haouas, I., Sayre, E., & Yagoubi, M. (2012). Youth unemployment in Tunisia: Characteristics and policy responses. *Topics in Middle Eastern and African Economies, 14*, 395–415.

Hunt, P. (2009). The locus of Carthage: Compounding geographic logic. *African Archaeological Review, 26*, 137–154.

Index Mundi (2012). Tunisia Economy Profile. Retrieved from http://www.indexmundi. com/tunisia/economy_profile.html

Inkseep, S. (2012, June 7). Tunisia's leader: Activist, exile and now president. National Public Radio. Retrieved from http://www.npr.org/2012/06/07/154430397/tunisias-leader-activist-exile-and-now-president

International Foundation for Electoral Systems. (2011). National Constituent Assembly election results announced in Tunisia. Retrieved from http://www.ifes.org/Content/Publications/News-in-Brief/2011/Nov/National-Constituent-Assembly-Election-Results-Announced-in-Tunisia.aspx

Ministry of Higher Education and Scientific Research (MHESR). (2012). Higher education in features (2011–2012). Retrieved from http://www.mes.tn/anglais/donnees_de_base/2012/dep_an2011_2012.pdf

National Institute of Statistics—Tunisia: (2012) Most recent indicators. Retrieved from http://www.ins.nat.tn/indexen.php

Perkins, K. (2004). *A history of modern Tunisia*. Cambridge, UK: Cambridge University Press.

President's Commission on Higher Education. (1947). *Higher education for American democracy*. Washington, DC: U.S. Government Printing Office.

Profile: Zine al-Abidine Ben Ali. (2011, June 20). BBC. Retrieved from http://www.bbc. co.uk/news/world-africa-12196679

Shediac, R., Abouchakra, R., Moujaes, C. N., & Najjar, M. R. (2008). Economic diversification: The road to sustainable development. Retrieved from http://www.ideation-center.com/media/file/Economic_diversification2.pdf

TN-Médias. (2012). *A cause de la retenue sur salaires, protestation des instituteurs à Sidi Bouzid : Tunisie : Actualités : Tunisie : Tuniscope*. Retrieved from http://tn-medias.com/

2012/08/04/a-cause-de-la-retenue-sur-salaires-protestation-des-instituteurs-a-sidi-bouzid-tunisie-actualites-tunisie-tuniscope/

U.S. Department of State. (2012, August 17). U.S. relations with Tunisia. Retrieved from http://www.state.gov/r/pa/ei/bgn/5439.htm

U.S. Embassy, Tunis. (2012, April). ESF funding opportunity: University partnership. Retrieved from http://tunisia.usembassy.gov/esf-funding-april-10–2012.html

Wolf, A., & Lefévre, R. (2012, April 18). Tunisia: A revolution at risk. The Guardian. Retrieved from http://www.guardian.co.uk/commentisfree/2012/apr/18/tunisia-revolution-at-risk

World Bank. (2012). Tunisia overview. Retrieved from http://www.worldbank.org/en/country/tunisia/overview

LINDA SERRA HAGEDORN is professor and associate dean in the College of Human Sciences at Iowa State University in Ames, Iowa.

WAFA THABET MEZGHANI is an English for occupational purposes teacher at the Higher Institute of Technological Studies (ISET) in Sfax, Tunisia.

9

*The tumultuous events of the Arab Spring have challenged
higher education systems throughout the Middle East and
North Africa to become more responsive to citizens who
are impatient for change. Community colleges in the
United States can play a vital role in supporting much-
needed reforms. This article looks at the possibilities and
the challenges that community colleges in the United
States must anticipate as they develop new partnerships
in the region.*

U.S. Community Colleges and a Response to the Arab Spring

John W. Shumaker

Community Colleges and the Arab Spring

The dramatic political upheavals of the Arab Spring have resulted in new political dynamics in many Middle East and North Africa (MENA) nations. Beginning in December 2010, when initial protests broke out in Tunisia, popular discontent has focused on repressive governments, a lack of transparent democratic institutions, and massive unemployment. The unemployment crisis is especially critical among young people, and has underscored the urgent need for higher education systems in MENA countries to intensify efforts to produce graduates who have the knowledge, skills, and attitudes toward work that are demanded by the private sector. Employment in the public sector, once the assumed and preferred career path for university graduates, has become a less viable option, as governments have been compelled to downsize as a result of shrinking budgets. The consequence of this shift in employment patterns is a stark and perhaps counterintuitive new reality: The likelihood of unemployment in MENA countries actually *increases* as the level of education increases, and

---

The author is grateful for suggestions offered by Leslie Nucho, Vice President for Programs at AMIDEAST (Washington, D.C.), and Quincy Dermody, AMIDEAST Country Director in Tunisia, but accepts full responsibility for the accuracy of the text.

New Directions for Community Colleges, no. 161, Spring 2013 © 2013 Wiley Periodicals, Inc.
Published online in Wiley Online Library (wileyonlinelibrary.com) • DOI: 10.1002/cc.20052

113

the unemployment rate is now highest among young people who have completed a university degree (World Bank, 2008).

From 1970 to 2003, the 19 MENA countries were successful in increasing participation rates in higher education from 4.7% to 25.8% (World Bank, 2008), and rates were up from 20% to 30% between 2000 and 2008 (Jaramillo & Angel-Urdinola, 2011). However, national economies in MENA countries have not grown sufficiently to absorb the increased number of university graduates seeking employment. As a consequence, the number of unemployed university graduates has risen dramatically. The proportion of unemployed among university graduates in a selection of five MENA countries now ranges from 11% in Algeria to 14% in Tunisia, 22% in Morocco, 24% in the Palestinian Territories, and 43% in Saudi Arabia (O'Sullivan, Rey, & Galvez Mendez, 2011).

The problem of youth unemployment, especially among university graduates, has been long-standing throughout the MENA region; it reflects one of the well-documented and chronic weaknesses in many national higher education systems in the Arab world as a whole—the lack of alignment between university programs and the needs of the private sector. But that disconnect is only one of many persistent structural and systemic problems that have undermined the quality and effectiveness of higher education systems in MENA countries. These problems are well entrenched and have mostly resisted national and international efforts to fix them, despite what might appear to be countless interventions by international donors and higher education specialists. Many thorough institutional analyses by the World Bank (2008, 2012), *African Economic Outlook* (2012a), and independent studies by higher education specialists in the region and in the United States (Abdessalem, 2011; Choueiri, Choueiri, & Choueiri, 2012; "A Decade of Higher Education," 2010; El-Araby, 2011; Wilkens, 2011) agree on the fundamental problems. Among them are:

- Ministries of higher education that emphasize strong centralized management and control over policies, budgets, and institutional operations.
- Rigid and conservative university structures, policies, and management systems that limit the mobility and opportunities of students and constrain entrepreneurial activity of creative faculty and universities.
- Large enrollment in social sciences and humanities and lower interest in science and technology (reflecting the assumed career path into the public sector).
- Low quality and lack of rigorous assessment systems.
- Misalignment between university programs and priorities and the needs of the private sector or national economies.
- Weak linkages between universities and the private sector.

As noted later, there have been some encouraging signs of nascent reform efforts at the national or system level in several MENA countries (e.g., Morocco, Tunisia, Jordan), but some of the most interesting and effective experiments have occurred at the institutional level—and many of these have involved U.S. community colleges. Eventually, however, the impetus and support for systemic change will have to involve the various national ministries. They—or governments of which they are a part—must create a policy framework and an environment for change that can stimulate and sustain much-needed national reforms. AMIDEAST is seeking to promote awareness among the region's higher education leaders and other stakeholders of the potential roles that partnerships with U.S. community colleges and universities can play in developing an environment conducive to reform.

The U.S. Community College as a Model for Reform

During the international Group of Eight (G-8) economic meetings in Washington, D.C., in May 2012, the Institute for International Education sponsored a summit on international education. Two of the speakers emphasized the growing importance of U.S. community colleges to international development in higher education. U.S. Under Secretary of Education Martha Kanter reported that "the community college system is of great interest" in U.S. efforts to promote international education." And Adam Ereli, U.S. Principal Deputy Assistant Secretary of State for Educational and Cultural Affairs, indicated that a growing number of countries are looking at the U.S. community college model as a way to meet their needs for skilled workers (*Community College Times*, 2012).

There is abundant evidence that the U.S. community college concept has gained significant traction in many MENA countries, and many individual U.S. community colleges have served as partners in adapting that concept to the needs of local institutions in several countries. For example, LaGuardia Community College in New York partnered with Universidad Central de Chile to create the Community College of Santiago, and students who complete a 2-year degree can transfer credits to the university if they opt not to enter the job market immediately. Houston Community College is providing technical assistance to Qatar Community College, and Community Colleges for International Development, a leader in promoting international engagement among community colleges, has helped to establish community colleges in the Republic of Georgia and in Madras, India. And there are several other individual community college development projects under way in Jordan, Egypt, and Morocco (*Hechinger Report*, 2010).

Salmi (2009) argues that strong national economies depend on the existence of an *integrated* system of higher education composed of a variety of institutions that range from community colleges and polytechnics to world-class research universities. While the United States does not have a national system of higher education, one reason for the success of American higher education has been the evolution of an interconnected and collaborative network of different postsecondary options such as community colleges, technical colleges, 4-year colleges, and research universities in all 50 states. The process of bringing these institutions together has required decades of debate, policy changes, legislative mandates, and reform to achieve. While the results are neither perfect nor complete, the growth and development of more than 1,200 community colleges in the United States after World War II has been a major factor in creating an increasingly seamless network of tertiary education institutions that has produced a form of quality postsecondary study available to practically anyone who wants it—regardless of educational background—in every state. This synergy has been a major factor in promoting highly creative approaches toward workforce development, economic growth, technology transfer, entrepreneurship, partnerships with business, and lifelong learning in American higher education.

Many aspects of the U.S. community college model are clearly relevant to the needs of the MENA region, and are uniquely positioned to act quickly and creatively to help postrevolutionary governments to respond to the demands of impatient citizens. Ministries of education do not have the luxury of time for protracted theoretical or abstract arguments about new models of higher education. They face an immediate need to implement practical reforms that will make higher education more directly responsive to national problems and priorities and to individual demands. Citizens want tangible and meaningful results, not endless political debates. They expect higher education systems and institutions to focus on solving the widespread problem of youth unemployment, to broaden the range of educational opportunities available to citizens for whom any form of postsecondary education has been out of reach, and to become more effective partners with government and the private sector to stimulate economic growth. While universities in the United States and Europe have much to offer to universities in the MENA region and elsewhere, it is the U.S. community college—nimble, flexible, effective, open, and intensely focused on the needs of students and communities—that can offer the most innovative and practical possibilities for national ministries and institutions to consider and adapt rapidly to a new political and economic environment.

New Technical Institutes and Community Colleges

Some MENA countries had taken steps to address these problems before the dawn of the Arab Spring and have developed community colleges to offer technical or career-related programs that lead to specialized diplomas or terminal undergraduate degrees. Beginning in the 1990s, Tunisia established an extensive national network of 24 new Higher Institutes of Technological Studies (*Instituts Supérieurs des Etudes Technologiques*, or ISETs) to address the need for a stronger link between higher education and employment in technology-based fields. As a result, according to the

African Economic Outlook (2012b p. 14), "82% of ISET graduates (over 7,900) have found jobs within six months of graduation, while another 9% have gone on for further study" (p. 14). And linkages with the private sector for program development, innovation, entrepreneurship, and practical training seem to be increasing more rapidly in Tunisia than elsewhere in the region (TEMPUS, 2010; World Economic Forum, 2011).

In 1992 the government of Yemen launched a feasibility study of the possibility of creating a community college system. In 1998, a presidential decree in Yemen established the Community College of Sana'a. The college opened its doors in 2001 with an emphasis on applied sciences, engineering, and management (http://www.scc.edu.ye). Since then, new community colleges focusing on technical fields have opened in Yemen at Aden, Seiyun, and Sanhan. Community colleges have existed in Jordan since 1981, where there are at least 51 such institutions (many of which are private and for-profit) that focus on career-related programs (TEMPUS, 2012).

It is important to note, however, that many of these institutions emphasize preparation for technical careers and do not offer the rich menu of programs, services, and educational opportunities available at U.S. community colleges. For example, community colleges in Yemen and Jordan do not follow an open admissions policy common at U.S. community colleges, they do not appear to have a robust system of student support to help students succeed, and they do not (except perhaps in the case of Sana'a Community College in Yemen) have programs to serve students who have not completed work at other institutions. In Yemen, there seems to be little opportunity for graduates of community colleges to advance to university study. Jordan, in contrast, has made provision for some students to transfer to university programs provided that they pass the required comprehensive examination that all community college students must pass to receive a diploma and satisfy other requirements. And the Ministry of Higher Education has developed bridging regulations to govern the transfer of credits (TEMPUS, 2012).

In 2009, as part of the Broader Middle East and North Africa program—launched in 2004 by the Group of Eight industrialized nations—Higher Education for Development (HED; www.hedprogram.org) began its U.S. Community College Small Grants Initiative to stimulate collaboration between several U.S. community colleges and technical institutions in the MENA region with a goal of promoting workforce development and entrepreneurship in Egypt, Jordan, and Morocco. In June 2012, USAID and HED expanded the program to emphasize entrepreneurship and include five more institutions and several additional U.S. community colleges. In addition, USAID and HED have sponsored many impressive projects involving U.S community colleges and institutions throughout the MENA region that merit attention as informative examples of successful partnerships that demonstrate the great potential of community colleges to make significant contributions to international development.

In 2011 USAID funded a project to determine the feasibility of establishing community colleges in Egypt. The focus of the study is first to determine if the policies and structures of the higher education system as a whole would support the creation of these new institutions and then to identify possible policy and regulatory reforms necessary to enable them to thrive and be sustainable. This study will address important systemic issues that are relevant to the creation of U.S.-style community colleges throughout the MENA region (https://www.fbo.gov/index?s=opportunity&mode=form&tab). HED facilitated a partnership in agriculture among Walla Walla Community College, Al-Azhar University in Egypt, and business partners in both countries that emphasizes an assessment of technical skills, skills standards, curriculum development, and teacher training (http://www.hed-program.org).

There have also been encouraging signs of additional progress over a broad range of workforce development issues elsewhere in the MENA region. In Jordan, recent higher education reforms have increased the level of private-sector participation on the national Council of Higher Education, and universities have begun to engage representatives of the private sector in campus job fairs to link students to employment opportunities. They have also formed alumni associations to support students in their search for employment (TEMPUS, 2012).

In Morocco there are several networks promoting collaboration between universities and the private sector, and the Ministry of Higher Education has actively promoted the creation of technology transfer, incubation centers, and innovation strategies that involve interaction between universities and the business sector (TEMPUS, 2010b). The most recent Action Plan of the Ministry (2013–2016) includes a substantial investment in strengthening partnerships between higher education and the private sector. It also emphasizes the need to encourage and increase enrollments in career-related fields that reflect national economic priorities.

National Symposium on Tunisian Higher Education and U.S. University Engagement

Tunisia's Ministry of Higher Education and Scientific Research has recently begun to look more closely at higher education in the United States for new ideas following the revolution of January 2011. In early November 2012, the Ministry and AMIDEAST collaborated to organize a symposium on Tunisian higher education and U.S institutional engagement. Approximately 60 university presidents, senior administrators, faculty, and private-sector representatives from Tunisia attended over the course of the 2-day event. The agenda focused on four areas of strategic interest in the Ministry: leadership and governance, community colleges and ISETs, work-integrated learning, and faculty development for teaching and learning. The choice of topics reflects ongoing interest in the critical areas of potential higher education reform: unemployment among university graduates; misalignment between university graduates and the needs of employers; greater emphasis on career services for students and graduates—including internships and cooperative education; improvement of teaching and learning; and stronger functional linkages among higher education, the private sector, and a variety of other important stakeholders.

The symposium confirmed that there are many aspects of the U.S. community college and university experience that can be useful to Tunisia as it develops options for reforming its higher education system. At the same time, however, the discussions quickly identified important differences between the role and function of the Tunisian ISETs and those of the U.S. community college. As clearly stated in this volume's chapter by Hagedorn and Mezghani, admission to the ISETs is based on merit as determined by the score on the national baccalaureate examination; the ISETs offer terminal undergraduate degrees (*licences*) in technical and managerial fields—and there is even some speculation about the possibility of offering some applied master's degrees. The ISETs are not closely linked to Tunisia's 13 universities or purposes of academic collaboration, and opportunities for transfer are limited to some top students; neither are they tasked with providing expanded educational opportunities for the public at large, although their legal framework does permit them to offer specialized training for companies in their communities.

The Challenges Ahead

There are many fundamental differences between higher education systems in the MENA region and those in the United States. Within the MENA region there are multiple challenges in response to impatient youth demands as well as for programs that serve the needs of national economies. Some of these challenges are systemic and fall within the purview of the government and the relevant ministry to resolve. International partners, such as American-style community colleges, can be useful technical resources to support efforts for reform. Others, however, are campus-based and more amenable to creative experimentation at a local level, and might eventually stimulate or support discussions about change and reform at the national level. Regardless of their type, mutual awareness of both national and local issues as well as differences between U.S. and MENA partners is necessary background to any collaboration between U.S. community colleges and MENA universities or community colleges. A representative sample of both system- and institution-based issues is provided next.

Three Systemic Issues

The slow pace of change in higher education in MENA countries reflects a mix of complex economic, social, and political issues that will require time, patience, and spirited national debate to resolve. Current higher education systems and polices are deeply rooted in the values, traditions, and practices of pre-revolutionary governments. As a generation of new leaders begins to look closely at other national systems in hopes of improving their own, they will find many major challenges that require action at a national level to create a framework for meaningful reforms at both the system and university levels.

Higher Education Governance: Centralized Control Versus Institutional Autonomy. Strong centralized control of universities is a vestige of centralized national governance that prevailed in most MENA countries prior to the Arab Spring. In Tunisia, for example, the legacy of the prerevolutionary government places the Ministry of Higher Education in a commanding position over all higher education institutions and operations. Tunisia's (prerevolution) higher education law of 2008 includes provisions to promote greater autonomy and flexibility for institutions, and the new leadership of the Ministry seems genuinely committed to implementing this important change over time; the actual decrees necessary to implement the law have been approved but not yet put into effect.

Centralized governance can provide powerful leadership and support for significant reform. A strong, visionary ministry can take bold steps to encourage a national debate about the mission and strategic development of higher education; it can invite participation of university leaders in policy discussions, gradually increase the autonomy and operational flexibility of universities and technical institutes, enhance the ability of newly elected university presidents to respond quickly and creatively to the needs of students and the private sector, welcome major stakeholders to participate in policy debates, and encourage open discussion about alternative approaches to higher education that might involve controversial reforms.

Leadership. One of the most important changes in higher education in Tunisia resulting from the revolution of 2011 was a new policy that mandates the election of university presidents and deans rather than their appointment by the central government. This change has the potential to infuse universities with new energy and optimism. At the same time, however, it has catapulted a group of successful professors into a new role for which, many readily acknowledge, they are unprepared. At this point many observers note that the new presidents' job remains one of serving as the Ministry's administrative representatives on the campus and having little independent authority to lead and manage institutional change.

This situation has slowed the process of granting autonomy and flexibility to universities and ISETs. The Ministry makes a valid point in stating that those newly elected university leaders do not yet have the capacity to administer their institutions—to say nothing of leading major changes. The presidents, in turn, note the absence of any training or professional development programs that might better prepare them or other campus leaders to handle the authority and responsibilities that will come with increased autonomy. As reform movements take hold in other MENA countries, the issue of how to identify and develop a new generation of higher education leaders will inevitably arise.

The goal of making colleges and universities more responsive to national needs and listening to major stakeholders, including the public, will require ministries, the universities, and community colleges and technical institutes to confront the enormous challenges that major reforms will present. This challenging task will require capable and focused leadership at every level to direct and manage significant changes in the higher education system. New presidents and their senior staffs will, of course, require systematic exposure to technical information and international good practices in key areas of management, but they would also benefit from broader discussions of evolving concepts of leadership and how to manage large-scale institutional and systemic change. Forward-looking ministries can lead such an effort in executive capacity development and then take steps to empower campus leaders to lead similar efforts at their own institutions.

Eventually it will be necessary for ministries of higher education throughout the MENA region to design a sustained program of practical (not theoretical) leadership development for university presidents and executive staff that will prepare them for their new roles and responsibilities. Open and inclusive discussion about mission, values, and priorities for higher education would be a good starting point for such an exercise. Far from being an abstract theoretical exercise, this type of sustained and open interaction in Tunisia among ministry officials and university leaders would be practically unprecedented in the Arab world. It would result in a new conceptual framework for university development and be a powerful stimulus for change for higher education in the entire MENA region. This change will occur more rapidly in some countries than in others, and in some it might be impossible. But it is likely that those systems that move decisively in the direction of autonomy and a new paradigm of institutional leadership will advance more quickly to make institutions more responsive to urgent national needs.

Many U.S. community colleges, universities, professional associations, and other educational organizations—including Iowa State University, the University of Texas, the American Council on Education, the American Association of Community Colleges, and AMIDEAST—have developed splendid leadership development programs for presidents, vice presidents, and deans that can be adapted to higher education in all MENA countries that are committed to genuine reform.

Access and Flexibility.   Higher education systems in the MENA countries are centrally managed by ministries that control an admissions system that is rigidly hierarchical in structure and strictly merit based. Pathways for higher education are limited on the basis of the score on the national comprehensive examination administered to secondary school graduates. A score below 60% will often remove the option of any university study except at a private (usually for-profit) institution, where fees can become an insurmountable obstacle. A student who blossoms after two or more years of postsecondary study—or who is above a maximum age limit—will have few options for additional higher education. Neither are there many opportunities for lifelong learning for personal or professional development.

By contrast, the rapid development of the U.S. community college system after 1945 involved a uniquely American commitment to the concepts of access and excellence. It was the final link in the creation of a seamless continuum of opportunity for new generations of students who were not served by traditional 4-year colleges and universities. The community college system opened the door for any student—regardless of age, academic background, employment status, or economic circumstances—to enter the country's higher education system.

As a result of the evolution of the U.S. community college, American higher education has become the most open, flexible, and student-centered system in the world. At its most flexible—at both the community college level and the university level—it permits students to change programs and majors, to transfer from one university or community college to another (or back again), stop out and return, study part-time or full-time, earn credits online, or combine credits from several institutions to obtain a fully accredited degree. The U.S. community colleges can show how an open system, one that emphasizes open access, flexibility, and unlimited opportunity, actually works in practice.

Four Institutional Issues

The process of national and system reform need not, however, prevent individual universities and effective academic and administrative leaders from introducing new strategies and practices to improve services to students, to stakeholders, and to communities. Among the most useful options for such campus-based innovation and reform are significant stakeholder engagement, focus on students and their success, emphasis on application rather than theory, and effective teaching and learning.

Significant Stakeholder Engagement.   Formal governance bodies— or independent buffer agencies (Fielden, 2008) to which the government has transferred responsibility and authority for governance and oversight of institutions—are not the rule in government-controlled higher education systems in MENA countries. But colleges and universities in the region can perhaps take some small initiatives on their own and begin engaging stakeholders as regular advisers and interlocutors in aspects of planning, development, and accountability at the campus level. Such experiments can perhaps set an example for a ministry that is not accustomed to open and inclusive engagement with important stakeholders. As things now stand, it appears that key stakeholders in the region are beginning to play an increasing role as advisers to academic programs in technical fields. It is true in

Tunisia's ISETs (TEMPUS, 2010) and in Jordan (TEMPUS, 2012), and is growing in Morocco (TEMPUS, 2010b).

At the same time, however, in none of these countries are there strong, independent governance or advisory bodies in place to guide the development of higher education planning and policy at the system or institutional level. The ministry remains a strong central authority that is closed to formal and systematic interaction with key stakeholders. Moreover, national higher education councils, even if they have authority or strong influence over important aspects of higher education, are usually composed mainly of university presidents or academics and have no members from the private sector, civic organizations, faculty, alumni, or students. One key factor in the success of the U.S. higher education system as a whole is its openness to full participation of key stakeholders—and especially representatives of the private sector—in governance, planning and development, quality assurance, advocacy, and resource development. Active and extensive engagement of stakeholders increases community understanding of the value of a strong college or university and serves as a source of advice, political support, practical insight, and opportunities for faculty and students to link their skills to specific local needs and priorities.

The engagement and the support of diverse stakeholders are dynamic and pervasive at the U.S. community college (as at most other U.S. colleges and universities, whether public or private). Community colleges *belong* to their local constituents and institutions. In most cases they are governed by local boards of trustees that represent community interests on a daily basis in a direct and personal way that is not possible at large national or regional universities. In addition, community colleges welcome community representatives to serve on a variety of advisory committees that have an important voice in campus life, and experienced professionals from the community often serve as part-time instructors to bring a practical perspective to the students' academic experience. This high-level local engagement and dedication—coupled with governance systems that emphasize local autonomy and management flexibility—enables a community college to identify and respond quickly to local concerns and to get rapid feedback on the quality and effectiveness of its activities. Colleges and universities in MENA countries recognize the value of such relationships, but lack policies and structures to take full advantage of them.

The U.S. community college can explain and demonstrate many examples of how extensive involvement of major stakeholders and community organizations can strengthen and energize an institution. They also can provide practical examples of the many types of partnerships with local organizations that not only enrich the educational experience of students but also enhance their opportunities for employment after graduation. And community college presidents can contribute to the professional development of their Tunisian counterparts by introducing them to the strategies and dynamics of community engagement.

A Focus on Students and Their Success.   Active concern for or substantial investment in the success of students is not evident at most MENA colleges and universities. A significant percentage of students who begin a university program do not graduate. These numbers represent a significant waste of human capital and government resources. To abandon these students without providing them with other educational opportunities results in a poorly educated, untrained, and frustrated workforce that is not qualified to participate meaningfully in the complex knowledge economy that Tunisia and other MENA countries aspire to develop. This unfortunate by-product of a restrictive higher education system is a major contributing factor to the large number of unemployed youth throughout the MENA region—especially when added to the high level of unemployment among those who do in fact complete their program.

U.S. community colleges have embraced a philosophy that emphasizes opportunity for all and an active commitment to the success of students. They recognize that a student's failure might in fact result from many factors, some the responsibility of students but others that are perhaps the consequence of an unresponsive, unsupportive, or uncaring institution. To an increasing extent, therefore, U.S. universities are investing heavily in a variety of student support programs and services designed to increase the chances of a student's success and eventual employment. American universities and community colleges are willing to accept the possibility that the failure of some students to complete a degree may be as much the fault of the institution as of the student. In fact, state governments, the media, and trustees in the United States have made improved retention and graduation rates an important indicator of institutional quality and effectiveness.

Theory Versus Application.   A recent analysis by the World Bank (2012) provides an interesting case study of how the emphasis on theory in curriculum development and course design and teaching in Tunisia impedes the teaching capacity of professors and impoverishes the learning experience of students. It also illustrates how the lack of practical insight and experience diminishes the employability of even the brightest graduates.

There are encouraging signs in the MENA region of increased interaction among universities, ISETs, and the private sector in the development of academic and training programs, student assessment, and the development of career services (TEMPUS, 2012). Study of the U.S. community college system will reveal the significant impact of putting theory and knowledge to work as an institutional priority, also revealing the value of such work-integrated learning strategies as internships and cooperative education as well as career development services.

Community colleges also provide a wide array of services to businesses and community organizations as part of their core mission to provide direct support for economic development by responding to the needs of local enterprises, providing vocational as well as academic and preprofessional education, contract education, consulting services, support of entrepreneurs and new business start-ups, and preparation for initial entry or reentry into a college or university. Community colleges in the United States are full-service centers for many types of education, information, or consulting needs identified by the local community.

U.S. community colleges can provide specific examples of how linking theory and practice actually works. They can also demonstrate the importance of programs involving work-integrated learning; cooperation with stakeholders; and partnerships with local businesses, civic organizations, and government to their success in promoting workforce development and economic growth.

Teaching and Learning. Tunisian ISETs, community colleges in Yemen and Jordan, and technical institutes across the MENA region are fundamentally teaching institutions. The importance assigned to teaching suggests they all could benefit from an investment in developing faculty to be inspiring and effective teachers and in designing ways to improve and document learning as an important indicator of institutional effectiveness.

Universities in Egypt, Lebanon, and Palestine have made a significant commitment to developing the capacity of faculty members to be effective teachers, to support them in the creation or redesign of courses or curricula to focus on active learning, to develop new methods of assessing students' performance, and to develop new opportunities for problem-based or community-based learning. These programs have also stimulated the development of new areas of applied pedagogical research as well as professional associations that enable faculty members to share ideas about academic development, to exchange course materials and debate new approaches to teaching, to explore the possibilities and implications of e-learning, and to interact with international specialists in teaching and learning from around the world. Specialized centers for teaching and learning at the American University of Beirut, the American University in Cairo, and An-Najah National University and Bethlehem University in Palestine are splendid paradigms for how such programs work at MENA universities.

The U.S. community college can provide a variety of examples of effective teaching and learning practices and programs that might be useful for their regional partners to consider as a way to enhance the capacity of faculty members to function as effective teachers and perhaps to increase the employability of students by involving the private sector and other community-based organizations in the development of curricula and as instructors with a practical orientation.

Possibilities for the Future

As U.S. community colleges and universities find their experience to be increasingly relevant to higher education reform efforts in the Middle East and North Africa, they will discover abundant opportunities to develop linkages and partnerships with national systems that want to learn from

NEW DIRECTIONS FOR COMMUNITY COLLEGES • DOI: 10.1002/cc

their success. But they will also encounter long-held traditions, assumptions, and practices in higher education that are incompatible with their own and that will be difficult to change quickly. This brief summary covers only a few of the core issues that can affect such partnerships and that must be approached with open eyes at the outset of collaborative programs.

There are several possibilities for collaborative projects at the system level that can involve universities and community colleges in the United States. Among them are the following:

- A national roundtable series on the mission, structure, and quality of higher education system. This is necessary in most (if not all) MENA countries. Roundtables should be open to the public and include higher education leaders as well as broad representation of key stakeholders. Sessions will focus on reaching a national consensus on the strategic direction and plan for the system. They can also offer a forum for stakeholders to address the systemic and institutional challenges that require open debate as a way to forge a national consensus about the strategy and priorities for reform. As a result of these discussions, the relevant ministry can appoint a number of task forces to follow up on key issues and recommend specific action plans for implementation of new initiatives.
- A leadership development program for campus presidents and senior staff—as well as ministry staff—to identify their interests and needs and to design a series of programs and activities in response. A major role of higher education leadership is to lead and manage change. Although higher education reform will certainly require leadership at the national and ministerial level, it will also depend on the availability and commitment of visionary and effective institutional leaders who can inspire and support others to embrace the quest for ways to make institutions better and more effective. The creation of a national or regional program for higher education leadership to serve all ministries and institutions could have a dramatic impact not only in MENA countries but on higher education systems throughout Africa and the Arab world.
- Systematic national efforts to promote improvements in teaching and learning. Whether in the form of a national center, institutional centers, or a combination of the two, ministries and stakeholders should sponsor planning and implementation of these centers to create a national community of practice dedicated to improving the environment for the success of students.

U.S. universities and community colleges can serve as important resources to support these and other efforts aimed at promoting reforms that will enable higher education systems in the MENA region to respond effectively to the urgent priorities of citizens who have been given new hope by the Arab Spring. AMIDEAST is prepared to serve as a resource across the MENA region through its national offices and staff as well as in conjunction with its large network of resources in government, the private and civil sectors, and the education community.

References

Abdessalem, T. (2011). Scope, relevance and challenges of financing higher education: The case of Tunisia. *Prospects (UNESCO)*, *41*, 135–155.

African economic outlook 2012: Promoting youth employment. (2012a). Paris, France: OECD Publishing.

African economic outlook 2012: Tunisia. (2012b). Paris, France: OECD Publishing.

Choueiri, E., Choueiri, G., & Choueiri, B. (2012). University governance and autonomy in the changing landscape of higher education. *Report of the 4th International Conference of the Arab Organization for Quality Assurance in Education*, 322–334.

Community college times. (2012, May 4). Washington, DC: American Association of Community Colleges.

A decade of higher education in the Arab states (1998–2009): Achievements & challenges (regional report). (2010). In B. Lamine (Ed.), *Towards an Arab higher education space* (pp. 11–58). Beirut, Lebanon: UNESCO.

El-Araby, A. (2011). A comparative assessment of higher education financing in six Arab countries. *Prospects (UNESCO)*, *41*, 9–21.

Fielden, J. (2008). *Global trends in university governance*. Washington, DC: World Bank.

Hechinger report. (2010, June 26). New York, NY: Teachers College, Columbia University.

Jaramillo, A., & Angel-Urdinola, D. (2011). Higher education, productivity, and labor market insertion. In *Breaking even or breaking through: Reaching financial sustainability while providing high quality standards in higher education in the Middle East and North Africa*. Washington, DC: World Bank.

O'Sullivan, A., Rey, M.-E., & Galvez Mendez, J. (2011). Opportunities and challenges in the MENA region. In *The Arab world competitiveness report, 2011–2012*. Geneva, Switzerland: World Economic Forum/OECD.

Salmi, J. (2009). *The challenge of establishing world class universities*. Washington, DC: World Bank.

TEMPUS. (2010a). *Higher education in Lebanon*. Brussels, Belgium: Education, Audiovisual, and Cultural Executive Agency (EACEA).

TEMPUS. (2010b). *Higher education in Morocco*. Brussels, Belgium: Education, Audiovisual, and Cultural Executive Agency (EACEA).

TEMPUS. (2012). *Higher education in Tunisia*. Brussels, Belgium: Education, Audiovisual, and Cultural Executive Agency (EACEA).

TEMPUS. (2012). *Higher education in Jordan*. Brussels, Belgium: Education, Audiovisual, and Cultural Executive Agency (EACEA).

Wilkens, K. (2011). *Higher education reform in the Arab world*. Washington, DC: Brookings.

World Bank. (2008). *The road not travelled: Education reform in the Middle East and Africa*. Washington, DC: World Bank.

World Bank. (2012). Investing in Tunisia's higher education system. In *Tunisia: From revolution to institutions*. Washington, DC: International Bank for Reconstruction and Development/World Bank.

World Economic Forum. (2011). Capitalizing on Africa's resources. In *The Africa competitiveness report*. Geneva, Switzerland: World Economic Forum.

JOHN W. SHUMAKER is chief of party of the USAID-funded Palestinian Faculty Development Program managed by AMIDEAST in the West Bank and Gaza.

INDEX

Statement of Ownership

Statement of Ownership, Management, and Circulation (required by 39 U.S.C. 3685), filed on OCTOBER 1, 2012, for NEW DIRECTIONS FOR COMMUNITY COLLEGES (Publication No. 0194-3081), published quarterly for an annual subscription price of $89 at Wiley Subscription Services, Inc., at Jossey-Bass, One Montgomery St., Suite 1200, San Francisco, CA 94104-4594.

The names and complete mailing addresses of the Publisher, Editor, and Managing Editor are: Publisher, Wiley Subscription Services, Inc., A Wiley Company at San Francisco, One Montgomery St., Suite 1200, San Francisco, CA 94104-4594; Editor, Arthur M. Cohen, ERIC Clearinghouse for Community Colleges, 3051 Moore Hall, Box 95121, Los Angeles, CA 90095; Managing Editor, Gabriel Jones, c/o UCLA Graduate School of Education, 2128 Moore Hall, Box 951521, Los Angeles, CA 90095-1521. Contact Person: Joe Schuman; Telephone: 415-782-3232.

NEW DIRECTIONS FOR COMMUNITY COLLEGES is a publication owned by Wiley Subscription Services, Inc. The known bondholders, mortgagees, and other security holders owning or holding 1% or more of total amount of bonds, mortgages, or other securities are (see list).

	Average No. Copies Each Issue During Preceding 12 Months	No. Copies Of Single Issue Published Nearest To Filing Date (Summer 2012)
15a. Total number of copies (net press run)	1,010	1,067
15b. Legitimate paid and/or requested distribution (by mail and outside mail)		
15b(1). Individual paid/requested mail subscriptions stated on PS form 3541 (include direct written request from recipient, telemarketing, and Internet requests from recipient, paid subscriptions including nominal rate subscriptions, advertiser's proof copies, and exchange copies)	426	415
15b(2). Copies requested by employers for distribution to employees by name or position, stated on PS form 3541	0	0
15b(3). Sales through dealers and carriers, street vendors, counter sales, and other paid or requested distribution outside USPS	0	0
15b(4). Requested copies distributed by other mail classes through USPS	0	0
15c. Total paid and/or requested circulation (sum of 15b(1), (2), (3), and (4))	426	415
15d. Nonrequested distribution (by mail and outside mail)		
15d(1). Outside county nonrequested copies stated on PS form 3541	127	128
15d(2). In-county nonrequested copies stated on PS form 3541	0	0
15d(3). Nonrequested copies distributed through the USPS by other classes of mail	0	0
15d(4). Nonrequested copies distributed outside the mail	0	0
15e. Total nonrequested distribution (sum of 15d(1), (2), (3), and (4))	127	128
15f. Total distribution (sum of 15c and 15e)	553	543
15g. Copies not distributed	457	524
15h. Total (sum of 15f and 15g)	1,010	1,067
15i. Percent paid and/or requested circulation (15c divided by 15f times 100)	77.4%	76.4%

I certify that all information furnished on this form is true and complete. I understand that anyone who furnishes false or misleading information on this form or who omits material or information requested on this form may be subject to criminal sanctions (including fines and imprisonment) and/or civil sanctions (including civil penalties).

Statement of Ownership will be printed in the Winter 2012 issue of this publication.

(signed) Susan E. Lewis, VP & Publisher-Periodicals